Storytelling in the Works of Bunyan, Grimmelshausen, Defoe, and Schnabel

The modern novel appeared during the period of secularization and intellectual change that took place between 1660 and 1740. This book examines John Bunyan's *Grace Abounding* and *The Pilgrim's Progress,* Johann Grimmelshausen's *Simplicissimus,* Daniel Defoe's *Robinson Crusoe,* and J. G. Schnabel's *Insel Felsenburg* as prose works that reflect the stages in this transition. The protagonists in these works try to learn to use language in a pure, uncorrupted way. Their attitudes towards language are founded on their understanding of the Bible, and when they tell their life stories, they follow the structure of the Bible, because they accept it as *the* paradigmatic story. Thus the Bible becomes a tool to justify the value of telling *any* story. The authors try to give their own texts some of Scripture's authority by imitating the biblical model, but this leads to problems with closure and other tensions. If Bunyan's explicitly religious works affirm the value of individual narratives as part of a single, universal story, Grimmelshausen's and Defoe's protagonists effectively replace the sacred text with their own powerful, authoritative stories. J. G. Schnabel illustrates the extent of the secularization process in *Insel Felsenburg* when he defends the entertainment value of escapist fiction and uses the Bible as the fictional foundation of his utopian civilization: arguments about the moral value of narrative give way to the depiction of storytelling as an end in itself. But Bunyan, Grimmelshausen, Defoe, and Schnabel all use positive examples of the transfiguring effect of reading and telling stories, whether sacred or secular, to justify the value of their own works.

Janet Bertsch teaches at Wolfson and Trinity College, Cambridge.

Studies in German Literature, Linguistics, and Culture

Edited by James Hardin
(*South Carolina*)

Storytelling in the Works of Bunyan, Grimmelshausen, Defoe, and Schnabel

Janet Bertsch

CAMDEN HOUSE

Copyright © 2004 Janet Bertsch

All Rights Reserved. Except as permitted under current legislation, no part of this work may be photocopied, stored in a retrieval system, published, performed in public, adapted, broadcast, transmitted, recorded, or reproduced in any form or by any means, without the prior permission of the copyright owner.

First published 2004
by Camden House

Camden House is an imprint of Boydell & Brewer Inc.
668 Mt. Hope Avenue, Rochester, NY 14620, USA
www.camden-house.com
and of Boydell & Brewer Limited
PO Box 9, Woodbridge, Suffolk IP12 3DF, UK
www.boydell.co.uk

ISBN: 1–57113–299–6

Library of Congress Cataloging-in-Publication Data

Bertsch, Janet, 1974–
    Storytelling in the works of Bunyan, Grimmelshausen, Defoe, and Schnabel / Janet Bertsch.
       p. cm. — (Studies in German literature, linguistics, and culture)
  Includes bibliographical references and index.
  ISBN 1–57113–299–6 (hardcover: alk. paper)
    1. Storytelling in literature. 2. German fiction—17th century—History and criticism. 3. German fiction—18th century—History and criticism. 4. Fiction—17th century—History and criticism. 5. Fiction—18th century—History and criticism. I. Title. II. Series: Studies in German literature, linguistics, and culture (Unnumbered)

PT275.B47 2004
833'.509—dc22

2004014262

A catalogue record for this title is available from the British Library.

This publication is printed on acid-free paper.
Printed in the United States of America.

To my sister, Heather

Contents

Acknowledgments	ix
List of Abbreviations	x
Introduction	1
1: Bunyan's *Grace Abounding to the Chief of Sinners*	7
2: Bunyan's *Pilgrim's Progress*	23
3: Grimmelshausen's *Der Abentheurliche Simplicissimus Teutsch* and *Der seltzame Springinsfeld*	47
4: Introduction to the *Robinsonade*	79
5: Defoe's *Robinson Crusoe*	89
6: Schnabel's *Wunderliche Fata einiger See-Fahrer (Insel Felsenburg)*	113
Conclusion	135
Works Cited	141
Index	147

Acknowledgments

THIS BOOK IS BASED ON material from two previous theses as well as more recent writing and research. I am grateful for the Killam Foundation's financial support, which permitted me to earn a master's degree at Dalhousie University, Halifax, Nova Scotia, Canada (1996–97). I owe thanks to all of the members of the Dalhousie German Department, above all to my supervisor, Professor Friedrich Gaede, and the departmental administrator, Gabrielle Wambold.

The Association of Commonwealth Universities funded my doctoral research for three years (1997–2000); the staff of the British Council also assisted in the administration of the award. At University College London, I received constant support and encouragement from my dissertation supervisors, Prof. Martin Swales and Dr. Adrian Stevens. Bill Abbey, the head librarian at the Institute of Germanic Studies, provided invaluable advice on many occasions. The comments of my two dissertation examiners, Dr. Jeffrey Ashcroft and Dr. Judith Hawley, have been extremely useful during the process of revising, reorganizing, and expanding this original material.

When I moved to Cambridge in 2002, the Faculty of English provided access to the Cambridge University Library. Although retired, Dr. Terry Llewellyn very kindly met with me for an illuminating chat about Grimmelshausen. He also read and discussed the final version of the manuscript. Professor Swales and Dr. Stevens have continued to be helpful and encouraging far beyond the call of duty, and I am very grateful for their practical and intellectual support throughout this project. The staff at Camden House, particularly Jim Hardin and Jim Walker, have also been very helpful. Finally, thanks are due to my husband, Daniel Morrison.

J. B.
June 2004

Abbreviations

FA   Defoe, Daniel. *The Farther Adventures of Robinson Crusoe Being the Second and Last Part of His Life*. London: William Clowes, 1974.

GA   Bunyan, John. *Grace Abounding to the Chief of Sinners*. Ed. Roger Sharrock. Oxford: Clarendon, 1962.

PP   Bunyan, John. *The Pilgrim's Progress from this World to That which is to Come*. Ed. J. B. Wharey and Roger Sharrock. Oxford: Clarendon, 1960.

RC   Defoe, Daniel. *The Life and Strange Surprizing Adventures of Robinson Crusoe of York, Mariner*. Ed. J. Donald Crowley. Oxford: Oxford UP, 1998.

SP   Grimmelshausen, Hans Jakob Christoph von. *Der seltzame Springinsfeld*. Ed. Franz Günter Sieveke. Tübingen: Niemeyer, 1969.

ST   Grimmelshausen, Hans Jakob Christoph von. *Der Abentheurliche Simplicissimus Teutsch und Continuatio des abentheurlichen Simplicissimi*. Ed. Rolf Tarot. Tübingen: Niemeyer, 1967.

WF   Schnabel, Johann Gottfried. *Wunderliche Fata einiger See-Fahrer*. 4 vols. Frankfurt am Main: Minerva, 1973.

Introduction

> Then they had them to some new places. The first was to *Mount-Marvel*, where they looked, and behold a man at a Distance, *that tumbled the Hills about with Words.*[1]

IN *GRACE ABOUNDING TO THE CHIEF OF SINNERS* (1666) and *The Pilgrim's Progress*, part 1 and part 2 (1678, 1684), John Bunyan tries to show his readers how to enter a world founded on the language and story of the Bible. Believers walk the path of righteousness by learning to read. They attain salvation by learning to tell their stories.

The seventeenth century was a time of religious upheaval and social and intellectual transition throughout Europe. Because of these political and ideological upsets, the seventeenth century also witnessed profound tensions in terms of language use and language theory. Medieval writers in the Augustinian tradition believed that there is an inherent, God-given correspondence between words and the things they describe, but new attitudes toward language and the process of signification emerged during the Reformation and Counter-Reformation. The central debates during the religious turmoil of the seventeenth century centered on questions concerning the status of biblical language, the authority of rival interpretations of the Bible, and the relationship between sign and meaning. Changing attitudes toward language resulted in changing attitudes toward reading and writing.

My analysis of works by two English and two German authors focuses on the impact of these attitudes toward reading, signification, and the Bible on the early modern novel. The following chapters discuss John Bunyan's *Pilgrim's Progress* and *Grace Abounding to the Chief of Sinners*, Hans Jakob Christoph von Grimmelshausen's *Der Abentheurliche Simplicissimus Teutsch* (Simplicissimus, 1668) and *Der seltzame Springinsfeld* (Springinsfeld, 1670), Daniel Defoe's *Robinson Crusoe* (1719), and the four volumes of Johann Gottfried Schnabel's *Wunderliche Fata einiger See-Fahrer* (The Island Felsenburg, 1731–43).

The initial goal of the protagonists of these works is to rediscover a use of language that is pure and direct, where words have a single, straightforward, divinely guaranteed meaning. The main characters in each of the books share a similar problem: human conduct does not always conform to Christian moral norms, nor does human experience always follow the paradigmatic structure of the Bible. The most effective way of learning to understand personal experience is to move beyond simple interpretation. Characters learn to tell their individual life stories to each other. These stories share a similar basic structure, use of language, and moral outlook. They thus contribute to the sense that a valid master narrative exists. The individual stories are variations on this single model.

If language and reading cause the problem, they also provide the solution. The protagonists in these texts resolve the gap between real life and biblical language by creating alternative, fictional communities bonded together by a shared vocabulary and the constant exchange of stories. Telling stories creates meaning because storytellers and readers or listeners agree about how to interpret and describe their experiences. This attitude toward communication approaches the modern idea that language is a process and that social consensus defines how words are used. Nonetheless, the way that these texts use storytelling to create meaning depends upon an understanding of the reading process that was common when they were written.

The medieval idea that reading and memorization transform the body and soul remained common into the early eighteenth century. The emphasis on affective reading that appeared during the Reformation and the Counter-Reformation strengthened the idea that texts transform their readers. According to Erasmus of Rotterdam, there is a unity between the educational and the entertaining experience of a text. The emotion created by reading or listening to a story moves the will and thus has a concrete moral effect on the reader or audience.[2] Martin Luther's faith in a self-interpreting Scripture privileges the book's ability to carry and create meaning above the interpretive and intellectual efforts of the reader.

The concept of experiential reading that appeared in the wake of German mysticism and pansophism during the seventeenth century[3] had a democratizing effect. The goal of mystic contemplation is to return to the unity between utterance and existence that characterized God's words during creation. The possession of a simple, unbiased heart makes readers receptive to religious illumination. Intellectual knowledge only obscures the relationship between the soul and God. The truth inherent in God's books, the Bible and the Book of Nature, can enter and affect the soul if readers empty their minds of preconceived notions and cultivate a passive and receptive attitude toward the truth the text contains. Well into the eighteenth century English sectarians and German pietists described the experience of reading the Bible as transcending the merely literal comprehension of the story. The Bible's power is to make its readers *feel* its truth, not just understand it intellectually. The Holy Spirit imprints the Bible's meaning into the hearts of believers.

Readers no longer view reading in the same way; as printed matter has become more common, they have learned to value it less. To a seventeenth-century English nonconformist or an eighteenth-century German pietist it was clear that the content of a story could be so moving, so sentimentally affecting, and so full of spiritual truth that it would simply seize its readers and *make* them believe. The authors discussed in this book reply to the seventeenth-century loss of confidence in the divinely determined meaning of Scripture with an ever-increasing emphasis on the power and authority of the sympathetic, emotional experience of the text. They are confident that stories told sincerely and with a serious moral purpose have the power to change their readers.

The common description of reading as "eating" a book reflects this older attitude toward reading. In *The Pilgrim's Progress* the feast at Gaius's inn uses the digestion metaphor to describe understanding and internalizing the lessons of the text. The root of the metaphor lies in the Book of Revelation (10:9), but it also appears in more secular contexts. In the *Book of Common Prayer*[4] and in Bunyan's work this metaphor applies to Scripture, but Phyllis Mack also mentions that seventeenth-century Quakers apply the digestion metaphor to learning more generally.[5] A similar secular use of the motif appears in the description of memorization in the comical *Lalebuch* of 1597.[6] A text, read and understood, becomes a part of the reader. The idea that reading actually alters the reader's will, intellect, and physical substance strengthens the normative and didactic impact of the text. In their capacity to provide mental refreshment or nourishment, books possess a power that is almost magical.

The four writers claim that their stories have a real value because the readers' emotional and sentimental responses to a work cause them to internalize its moral lesson. According to Grimmelshausen, Defoe, Schnabel, and even Bunyan in his allegory, the works may be fictional, but they have a moral value similar to or greater than real-life experiences. If the events in the texts did not occur, they really should have occurred and would have occurred if the world were not so corrupt. The truth of the stories matters less than their positive, ameliorative effect on their audience.[7]

The tension in these stories is unavoidable because of the gap between the secular/empirical and the spiritual realms that pervades seventeenth-century literature. Grimmelshausen, in particular, tries to justify his work by connecting it with the spiritual autobiography. He uses a retrospective narrator to provide religious commentary throughout *Simplicissimus*. At the same time, he describes a world of realistic details and strange occurrences that simply refuses to conform to a single, narrative model. While they risk exposing themselves to ridicule by writing imaginative works, all four authors also inherit the basic problem of the spiritual autobiography: How can personal experiences in a world that is corrupt, chaotic, and unstructured conform to a narrative model that demands that human experience demonstrate an underlying structure and meaning?

The general story of the Bible appears as the defining pattern for experience in the spiritual autobiography. Justifying the value of all of these texts depends on the fact that they try to imitate the structure of the Bible and reflect a specifically Christian set of moral and spiritual norms. By drawing parallels between the way their characters read the Bible and one another's stories, these authors claim the same affective qualities for their own texts. They refer to biblical teachings and use a loosely biblical structure in their works in order to substantiate their authority, their legitimacy, and their positive effects on the reader. In their most ideal and complete form, individual narratives re-create Scripture on a personal level by following the Bible so closely that they seem to become a part of that master text.

In relating a spiritual autobiography, an individual narrator learns to structure his or her story so that it follows the scriptural paradigm and learns to understand this story in the context of the divine plan for creation. The narrator thus defines himself or herself as a participant in a more comprehensive story written by God. By learning to tell their individual stories, the protagonists in the works of Bunyan, Grimmelshausen, Defoe, and Schnabel become the authors of their fates. They decide their futures by acting in the way that harmonizes best with how God wants them to act. Ideally, individual stories and God's plan share the same final goal, namely, returning to a prelapsarian state of perfect communication with God.

Although these four authors begin by affirming the authority of Scripture, they also tend to transfer the qualities that they attribute to Scripture to their own individual works. This causes a number of tensions. Part of the reason that closure becomes such a problem in these texts is that the biblical structure they follow has a very strong teleological impetus. The necessity of giving a definite ending to his works conflicts with Bunyan's theological position and creates many of the tensions in *Grace Abounding* and *The Pilgrim's Progress*. Bunyan moves from a focus on transcendent salvation in the first part to describing the community of believers in the second part out of a need to provide a satisfactory ending to his text.

The Bible is an extraordinary text because it claims to tell the entire history of creation and the history of mankind. As a story, it includes each and every one of its readers. The Bible tells its readers that history will end at the day of judgment, when the saved enter heaven and the damned go to hell. Its readers' individual fates are bound up in this comprehensive vision of human destiny. Because Grimmelshausen, like Bunyan, imitates the structure and the function of the Bible, his work also needs to reach an ending that is free of tension. To reach this satisfactory conclusion, however, he must foster the sense that the reader continues to participate in the text even beyond its happy ending. Simplicius's spiritually enlightened isolation at the end of the *Continuatio* thus gives way to the prosperous, inclusive community that appears in *Springinsfeld*.

The strength of the biblical paradigm is also responsible for the positive attitudes toward stories and storytelling that appear in the texts. Reading the Bible is an interactive process, and these authors urge their readers to participate in their texts in the same way. Bunyan includes marginal glosses in *The Pilgrim's Progress,* while Grimmelshausen and Defoe use retrospective commentary to provoke their readers' active interpretation of the text and enliven the reading process. To an even greater extent than the other authors, Schnabel includes examples of reading and storytelling in his work in order to heighten the sense that his book includes the reader within the community of narrators and listeners.

Modeling a narrative on the Bible — *the* paradigmatic story — creates a demand for completeness, comprehensiveness, and for an active interaction between the text and the reader. As an influence on the texts, the Bible's content becomes subservient to its status as a book. These texts actually become more secular because they try to imitate the Bible. They claim to lead readers to a salvation that is earthly and fictional, if not heavenly and spiritual. Protagonists become savior figures and effect a return to the Garden of Eden. They do this by learning to read their experiences and narrate them successfully. Thus, the process of reading and telling stories becomes sanctified as an end in itself.

These four authors attribute a power that is magical, transforming, and life-giving to the interaction between reader and text. Even when they appear most secular, these works retain their faith. It is a faith in the power of stories rather than a belief in the content of Scripture. At the same time that these authors are describing how difficult it is to maintain religious belief in a corrupt and chaotic world, they are creating an alternative reality through their fictions. Their stories affirm nothing less than the creative power and value of fiction itself.

Notes

[1] John Bunyan, *The Pilgrim's Progress from this World to That which is to Come*, ed. J. B. Wharey and Roger Sharrock (Oxford: Clarendon, 1960), 285. Subsequent references to this work are cited in the text using the abbreviation *PP* and page number.

[2] See Richard Waswo, *Language and Meaning in the Renaissance* (Princeton, NJ: Princeton UP, 1987), 229–30.

[3] In England the dissolution of censorship associated with the civil war resulted in the publication of numerous translations of German mystic and pansophic works, including books by Jakob Böhme (1645), Hendrik Niclaes (1646), and Valentin Weigel (1648). See Philip C. Almond, *Heaven and Hell in Enlightenment England* (Cambridge: Cambridge UP, 1994), 46.

[4] The reference appears in the Collect for the Second Sunday in Advent. See *The Book of Common Prayer, 1662* (Cambridge: Cambridge UP, 1968), 49.

[5] Phyllis Mack, *Visionary Women: Ecstatic Prophecy in Seventeenth-Century England* (Berkeley: U of California P, 1992), 135.

[6] Anon., *Das Lalebuch*, ed. Stefan Ertz (Stuttgart: Reclam, 1998), 71.

[7] See Wolfgang Kayser, *Die Wahrheit der Dichter: Wandlung eines Begriffes in der deutschen Literatur* (Hamburg: Rowohlt, 1959), 12.

1: Bunyan's *Grace Abounding to the Chief of Sinners*

JOHN BUNYAN'S SPIRITUAL AUTOBIOGRAPHY introduces many of the linguistic and religious tensions that appear in his fictional works, as well as those of Grimmelshausen, Defoe, and Schnabel. In *Grace Abounding to the Chief of Sinners* Bunyan tries to move from a reprobate existence to participate in the life and language of the righteous elect. This process is problematic, in part because of the conflict between his Calvinist theology and the structural demands of his source narrative, the Bible. An examination of *Grace Abounding* will clarify Bunyan's attitude toward language and the Bible and will highlight the difficult relationship between Bunyan's subjective reading and its goal, namely, the discovery of an objective, divinely ordained, hidden truth.

The protagonists in these chosen works experience two stages in the process of becoming storytellers. First they learn to interpret their experiences and then they learn to tell them to others. In *Grace Abounding* Bunyan describes how he learns to understand his personal experiences by learning to read the Bible. He provides positive evidence of his election by presenting his story as a narrative that agrees with biblical teaching, uses biblical language, and follows a loosely biblical structure.

In order to understand the importance of language and the Bible to Bunyan, it is necessary briefly to consider the importance of language in the religious developments of the sixteenth and seventeenth centuries. The central debates of the Protestant Reformation have a linguistic aspect. The translation of the mass and the Bible from Latin to the vernacular was central to the movement for ecclesiastical reform in both England and Germany. Protestant churches placed less emphasis on the signs and symbols of the communion service than on reading and interpreting the Bible. Literacy spread to a wider proportion of the population than ever before as a result of the invention of the printing press. Because of the Protestant emphasis on individual responsibility for salvation, the desire to read the Bible motivated many people to learn to read and write.

The Reformation also changed the way people read the Bible. Roman Catholic biblical hermeneutics recognized a whole series of different levels of meaning. These included various allegorical interpretations as well as typological readings of the New Testament. According to the typological reading, events from the New Testament answer the stories, symbols, and prophecies presented in the Old Testament by fulfilling, paralleling, or reversing them. Christ is the new Adam; the wooden cross reverses the Tree of Knowledge; the Virgin Mary counteracts the temptation of Eve. Reading the Old and New Testaments as a single, chronological story structured by typological correspondences generates an influential narrative pattern: the fall of man; a state of wandering, searching, and sin; salvation and the return to paradise.

During the Reformation and Counter-Reformation, the typological way of reading Scripture became more and more dominant. This also led to an increase in readings that applied elements of Scripture — particularly those in the Book of Revelation — to contemporary political and social occurrences. This historical typology is the central aspect of sixteenth- and seventeenth-century Protestant millenarianism. The English reformers and the Lutherans interpreted history in connection with the Bible, and vice versa.[1] English reformers under Elizabeth I emphasized the identity of the English nation with the chosen people of the Old Testament.[2] Both English and continental Protestant propagandists described the battle against Rome using images from the Book of Revelation. Reading the Bible could provide general knowledge concerning the spiritual inheritance of mankind, but it could also provide valuable information about present events.

For seventeenth-century nonconformists Scripture is the primary vehicle for communication from God concerning human redemption. The entire Bible can thus be read in a very personal way. Bunyan and his contemporaries apply the examples of characters in the Old and New Testaments to their own lives. The example of King David warns against the dangers of lust and illustrates God's punishment for indulging in the sins of the flesh.[3] Simon Peter and Judas show what happens to those who deny God; their individual stories illustrate variations in the degree of sin (*GA*, 46–47). Adam is an image of the sinful, carnal soul, while Christ is an image of the redeemed, spiritual soul. The entire chronology of the Old and New Testaments mirrors the drama the human soul experiences when it seeks salvation. The tendency to apply Scripture to the life of the individual means that the generalized chronology derived from a typological reading of the Old and

New Testaments becomes the influential structure for the spiritual autobiography.[4] According to seventeenth-century nonconformists, the life of every individual predestined for salvation conforms to this pattern. Each elect individual is born into sin, encounters a period of wandering and confusion, experiences redemption through Christ, and, finally, reaches the New Jerusalem.

What readers in a different, more secular era must realize is that to Bunyan the story presented in Scripture really was the sum of creation. For a person of humble birth, with limited access to printed resources, the stories of the Bible provided an explanation of the past as well as an important psychological framework for understanding the self in the present. Bunyan's sectarian doctrine, bolstered by works of popular devotional literature, affirms a specific set of interpretations of the Bible. The process of understanding Scripture is the process of understanding how the life of the individual conforms to these interpretations. A true understanding of the self extends the content of Scripture into every aspect of individual life through the system of analogies or parallels present in the personal/allegorical and typological readings. Because the redefinition of the self that accompanies this change of perspective is so complete, the authors of spiritual autobiographies frequently depict religious conversion as a moment of entry into a new land. This rebirth involves a complete transfiguration of the physical substance, sensory perceptions, patterns of thought, and language of the new convert.

The basic premise of Bunyan's autobiography is that only God sees creation as it truly is. Human limitations and corruption delude mankind. God provides signs to bring some individuals from a state of ignorance to a greater state of understanding. These signs are Christ's sacrifice, the words recorded in the Scriptures, and human experience. The better individuals learn to read and interpret these signs, the better they are able to harmonize their actions with God's purpose for creation. Because the command over language is a God-given tool to help man achieve salvation, the acts of swearing, lying, and blaspheming are wicked. Using words that do not mean what they say poses a fundamental threat to the existence of a single, divinely ordained system of signs. To use words in a loose or arbitrary fashion is to deny that there is any essential link between signs and their meanings.

The process of reconciling the self with God entails reading the single story told by historical events, the words of the Bible, and personal experience. By learning to interpret this story, elect individuals begin to understand what they should do and how they should act in order to reach its ending. The story ends when its reader attains salvation and enters heaven after having successfully reconciled the path of his or her life with the hidden plans of the divine author of creation.

Bunyan's search for correct interpretation, the proper connection between words and their meanings, is thus intimately linked to his search for God and his attempt to understand himself. He describes a process of generating new explanations and interpretations of his experiences as he tries to move from a life without meaning toward the assurance of salvation that will define his life completely. His account is, in a very real sense, the story of a man learning to read. He moves from a rudimentary ability to interpret characters to an ability to understand the subtleties of scriptural language and the connections between scriptural passages.

Readers of *Grace Abounding* may wonder why Bunyan places such an emphasis on the hidden meaning of the Bible and why he has to struggle so much to attain what he considers a correct interpretation of the story of Scripture. Why was it so difficult for Bunyan to understand what he read, given the fact that many popular devotional works of the time contain interpretations of the New Testament that agree with the main principles of Bunyan's Calvinist doctrine? Bunyan's interpretations rarely depart from what would have been acceptable to any of the nonconformist Protestant denominations. According to Bunyan, however, the Bible does not merely present a literal, historical tale. If the history it relates were the sum of the account, then God would save only the chosen people, the Israelites (*GA,* 9). Behind the words of Scripture lies the meaning of the Bible that transcends the letter: the experience of redemption through Christ. Like Martin Luther,[5] Bunyan emphasizes the strength of divine grace in grasping and convincing his passive soul.

In Bunyan's view the Bible cannot be understood properly by reprobate readers because its meaning actually needs to be felt and internalized. The words people speak and write on a daily basis are arbitrary and corrupt because they proceed from a corrupt creation. The Bible, however, is based in a single, essential, universal truth, namely, Christ as the Word of God. The lessons of Scripture have a universal significance ("Christ is the righteousness of all men") that at the same time conveys an intensely personal meaning ("Christ is *my* righteousness, he assures me of *my* salvation"). The grace afforded to the individual by Christ's sacrifice becomes the meaning behind all of the events of the Bible.

Bunyan is not just trying to understand the words of Scripture. Instead, he must learn to understand its meaning *for him*. As a member of the elect, he should live according to scriptural norms, and his life should become an example of the meaning that he has struggled to discern. Bunyan cannot say that he has understood the Bible in any sense until he has experienced Christ's imputed righteousness. He must recognize the significance of the universal story for his own personal redemption.

Bunyan must learn to speak as well as to read the Bible. He must tell his story using the same vocabulary and structure that other members of the elect use. Bunyan notices specific qualities in the speech of the pious. In his encounter with the poor people of Bedford, he remarks on the self-awareness of the speakers. They emphasize "*their* souls," "the work of God on *their* hearts," "how *they* were convinced," "with what words and promises *they* had been refreshed," "*their* own wretchedness of heart" (*GA*, 14; my italics). Their language derives its authority from personal experience rather than external institutions. It provides Bunyan with a vocabulary for the tumultuous and chaotic interior emotions that he has been unable to understand or control. Bunyan also remarks on the quality of their language: "And me thought they spake as if joy did make them speak: they spake with such pleasantness of Scripture language, and with such appearance of grace in all they said" (*GA*, 15). Their words share a common, irresistible motivation: joy *makes* them speak. The speakers have moved beyond merely reading Scripture to speaking through an internalized scriptural language. The personalized repetition and regeneration of Scripture through their mouths indicates the regeneration of their souls. They describe their experiences using scriptural images and words. Specific events, examples, and phrases provide paradigms for narrating experiences. Their way of reading the Bible also provides a general structure for telling their life stories. The common narrative model and shared vocabulary unifies and strengthens the community of the faithful.

As a language that describes feelings and emotions, the language of the elect is intimate and personal. As a language that uses a shared vocabulary to describe a similar set of experiences, it is also universal. The language of this community will ideally display few of the arbitrary meanings, deceptive qualities, and tendencies toward misinterpretation that characterize communication in the carnal world. Because there is a clear division between the damned and the saved, however, the language of the elect is also exclusive. As such, it can appear more forbidding than comforting.

Bunyan's vision of the poor people of Bedford sitting on the side of a mountain in the sun (*GA*, 19) demonstrates his anxiety concerning election and the exclusiveness of the language of the elect. In the vision, the difference between the sunny mountainside and the cold, dark area outside the wall shows the radical separation between the elect and the reprobate. The carnal world is the world that surrounds Bunyan. He seeks to enter the spiritual or redeemed world, but this requires a personal transformation and a concomitant change in perception and language. Bunyan glosses the wall as "the Word that did make separation between the Christians and the world" (*GA*, 20). His interpretation sheds light on the role of divine grace in creating understanding. Bunyan's description of the Word as the vehicle that separates the two worlds is at once logical and paradoxical. Understanding the story told by Scripture creates the separate and shared reality in which the poor people of Bedford dwell. Living according to the Bible is living in a different and exclusive realm. The inability to understand the Word, however, creates an insurmountable barrier to salvation, a wall that cannot be penetrated. The sense of hopeless exclusion so vividly described in the first paragraph of the vision is the despair of the damned. The Word appears threatening and forbidding because it is an indecipherable code to the reprobate individual.

The lesson of Bunyan's vision is that he must struggle to develop his understanding of Scripture in order to pass into the sunlight. Paradoxically, he can only develop a correct and full appreciation of the revealed meaning of the Bible passively. The narrow passage through the wall is "Jesus Christ," to whom Bunyan looks for the absolution of his sins. The reader's capacity to understand the Bible correctly depends on being called by Christ (*GA*, 24). It is impossible to reach a true understanding of the divine narrative without the help of divine grace, so the reader must be predestined for salvation before he can ever learn to read and speak in a way that does not separate him from God. Understood from a carnal viewpoint, the Bible is actually a barrier. It is full of dead and misleading signifiers that those who are predestined for damnation will never understand. The necessity of striving for salvation conflicts with the utter uselessness of such striving without divine assistance. The emphasis on the passivity of the reader and the indecipherable nature of the sacred text is responsible for much of the anxiety concerning reading and narrating that pervades *Grace Abounding*.

Because of his deep-seated paranoia regarding the signification process, Bunyan is careful to warn his readers about the dangers of misusing language. Hypocrisy and swearing are sinful, the former because the speaker intentionally uses words to disguise a truth and the latter because the speaker uses words in an arbitrary or defiant way. Since religious conduct implies a serious and considered use of signifiers, the misuse of words by professedly pious men is particularly fearful (*GA*, 7). He rejects bellringing and dancing as indulgent pleasures because they produce no useful or constructive results; they are examples of meaningless activity.

Bunyan also worries that perhaps truth does not exist, that it might be completely contingent on subjective definition. This explains his concerns about rival religious doctrines and ceremonies. The rhetoric of religion is very important to Bunyan. His quarrel with the mainstream Church of England is a quarrel over signification. Does spiritual meaning proceed from set, legislated forms of worship or from a sincere, interior conviction? Outward displays of godliness can cloak dissent and insincerity. Conversely, is there such a thing as religious belief that is too subjective, that has entirely lost its correspondence with the biblical narrative and the norms of the religious community? Like Christian in *The Pilgrim's Progress,* Bunyan must walk the narrow path between the hypocrisy of the Anglicans, whose actions and inner thoughts do not necessarily match their forms of worship, and the all-too-subjective Quakers (*GA*, 39). They reject all forms of signification, including the normative narrative of the Bible, in favor of a completely interior and individual understanding of religious illumination.

Bunyan is particularly careful to warn his readers against the antinomian theology of the Ranters (*GA*, 16). The Ranters are troublesome because they deny that words and actions have any objective meaning. They glory in the emptiness of all signs and the subjective nature of signification. When Bunyan's friend turns Ranter, he claims he has passed through various stages of interpreting Scripture, only to discover filthiness and uncleanness at the end (*GA*, 16). For Bunyan empirical experience reflects the active presence of God in the life of the individual. The Ranters believe they have reached a point of perfection where experience has no signifying value: they can do whatever they want and it makes no difference. In addition, the arbitrary subjectivity of Ranter behavior disregards the social consensus important to Bunyan's thought. The renegade use of language that appears in Ranter tracts, accompanied by a nihilism that feeds on the proliferation of meanings and expression, is anathema to Bunyan's search for stable and unambiguous signification.

To a great extent Bunyan's struggle for conversion is a struggle to develop his belief not in terms of a specific set of religious doctrines but in the capacity of language to convey *any* meaning. The ideas of the Ranters pose a particular threat to Bunyan because he suspects that words do not necessarily have a connection with their meanings. Because he is always aware of the deceptive potential of language, Bunyan has difficulty trusting the words of the people around him. At one point he even asks himself whether Paul made up the Bible to delude readers and lead them toward damnation. Paradoxically, the very power and authority of Paul's letters, his skill at using language, make it seem more likely to Bunyan that he possesses the ability to operate as an arch-deceiver (*GA*, 31). Bunyan's pessimism regarding human nature and his suspicions regarding the nature of words hamper his ability to place his faith in any system of meaning that claims to be true and definitive. The process becomes more difficult because of the proliferation of different types of religious belief and varying interpretations of Scripture. Although he tries to speak using the language of the godly and attempts to understand his own experiences according to what he has learned in the Bible, Bunyan's reading and speaking remain filled with tension throughout his autobiography.[6]

I have thus far outlined Bunyan's attitude toward the Bible and the language used by godly people in rather general terms. While I do not wish to provide a close reading of the entire text, I would like to discuss the preface and the conclusion to *Grace Abounding* in order to provide a more thorough and practical idea of how Bunyan actually wants language to work.

The introduction and the conclusion of Bunyan's autobiography proper demonstrate the level of understanding achieved by the author at the time of writing. *"The Philistians understand me not"* writes Bunyan in the preface to *Grace Abounding* (*GA*, 1). From the first he distinguishes between worldly language and the language of the converted. Bunyan uses the paradigm of Paul's epistles to address his audience.[7] He thus draws a connection between his individual account and a recognizable model from the Bible. In this he moves beyond mere simile. He does not quote biblical passages so much as speak them. They do not appear separately from his own words; he embeds scriptural phrases in his own sentences and links different passages together so that they fully describe his experiences. He speaks not *of* but *through* Scripture. Other nonconformists do the same thing,[8] and a similar use of metaphor appears in the various fictional texts discussed in this book. Bunyan uses metaphors taken from the Bible directly, without any added explanation, to illustrate his complete identification with the text. To justify writing the account, he draws on both Old and New Testament parallels. He applies Moses' command to remember the forty years in the wilderness to his own erring journey and once more invokes Paul's example. He shows his own reading abilities by using these examples. He can read the Old and New Testaments in terms of their thematic relation to each other; he can also understand how the experiences of specific figures apply to his own position.

Bunyan ends his preface with a comment on the style of his account that is important enough to be quoted at length:

> *I could have enlarged much in this my discourse of my temptations and troubles for sin, as also of the merciful kindness and working of* God *with my Soul: I could also have stepped into a stile much higher then this in which I have here discoursed, and could have adorned all things more then here I have seemed to do: but I dare not:* God *did not play in convincing of me; the* Devil *did not play in tempting of me; neither did I play when I sunk as into a bottomless pit,* when the pangs of hell caught hold upon me: *wherefore I may not play in my relating of them, but be plain and simple, and lay down the thing as it was.* . . . (*GA*, 3–4)

Bunyan does not view his use of metaphor primarily as an aesthetic achievement, as "play." Rather, he tries to eliminate gratuitous adornment in his speech and in his writing in order to maintain the basic connection between words and their meanings. Bunyan describes personal experience using metaphors taken from the Bible in order to affirm the connection between the two. The purpose of reading and writing is to create a harmony between the language of the individual and the language of God, between the life story of the individual and the story God tells through the Bible and the history of creation. The whole of *Grace Abounding* is concerned with the process of developing and maintaining the connections between the empirical realm and a hidden, divine truth through reading, writing, and narrating.

Bunyan also affirms the insights at which he has arrived in the paragraph that concludes the spiritual autobiography proper. In it he quotes and comments on the scriptural text that effects his final conversion, Heb. 12:21–23 (*GA*, 82). The quotation that comes to Bunyan so suddenly confirms Christ's call to him. As such, it provides a series of definitions that Bunyan can apply to his own identity. His uncertainty concerning his spiritual state is based equally on his inability to assess his own moral worth and his lack of insight into the workings of the divine plan. When the quotation appears to him as a revelation, it answers the specific questions concerning his own worthiness that he has repeated throughout the text. It confirms his election. The passage quells Bunyan's doubts so effectively because it includes an explicit statement of the relationship between the judgment of God the Father and the operation of grace that follows Christ's sacrifice (*GA*, 82). It reassures Bunyan that he may have escaped from his persistent fears of the rule of the law and damnation in favor of faith in divine grace and the possibility of salvation.

Like the preface, the conclusion of the autobiography proper has two functions. First, it illustrates the point of insight or understanding that Bunyan has reached at the time of writing the account. It affirms the authority or credibility of his perspective and attempts to provide a definitive, positive conclusion to his doubts and struggles. Second, it provides further insight into the proper way of reading and using language exercised by a member of the elect. Like a creed, the passage summarizes Bunyan's understanding of the Bible. He uses Old Testament references and prophecies (*"mount Zion," "Jerusalem"* [*GA*, 82]) typologically to describe the state of the elect; and he describes the rule of law in the context of its New Testament fulfillment. Bunyan's way of reading the passage demonstrates how he reads Scripture. Each and every word in the Bible possesses a definite truth. The sacred text has a certain power, an active, autonomous ability to reveal its meaning to the reader. Individual excerpts from Scripture contain a meaning that refers to the narrative as a whole, and they harmonize with each other. The meaning of Scripture — the lesson of how and why Christ redeems humanity — applies centrally to the life of the individual. Christ's death is an action of universal significance for all mankind, but the search for salvation is also the task of each individual, isolated Christian.

There is more to discovering how to speak the language of the blessed than simply learning how to read the Bible. In his preface Bunyan reflects at length on the importance of recalling and documenting personal experiences. By remembering his life, he is able to see the patterns in his spiritual development. Like Robinson Crusoe, Bunyan affirms the value of learning from mistakes. The memory of past dangers serves as a warning against the dangers of pride and complacency. Interpreted correctly, bad experiences play an important role during particular stages in the individual's spiritual journey — despair over personal sinfulness, for example, leads to the realization of the magnitude of divine grace — or teach specific lessons, as when Bunyan enumerates his sins and doubts and then lists the lessons they teach at the end of the account (*GA*, 102–3). It is even more useful to actually write out past experiences. The pattern of the narrative and its significance may be refined and reevaluated as time passes — witness Bunyan's numerous additions and emendations to the basic text of the autobiography — but the events themselves will not be lost in forgetfulness. As a stable, concrete account, the narrative also provides reassurance and assistance during periods of doubt or despair.

Bunyan's primary personal reason for writing *Grace Abounding* is to narrate the events of his life in a way that shows that he is a member of the elect. There is also a social reason for composing his life story. In the preface Bunyan underscores the intimacy of the relationship between the reader and the narrator by calling his readers *"children"* (*GA*, 1). Throughout the text the community of believers counterbalances the isolation of the individual in search of salvation. As the poor people of Bedford demonstrate, exchanging stories and accounts of conversion strengthens the faithful and encourages new believers.

The importance of the intersubjective or social element in Bunyan's text extends to the actual function of the narrative. In Restoration England nonconformist churches like the Bedford church possessed no institutional sanction, nor was their spiritual warrant generally recognized. These congregations justified their existence and based their authority on their members' shared reading of Scripture, exchange of conversion narratives, and interpretive consensus rather than from any outward acknowledgment by society as a whole. Sermons and discussions helped congregations to arrive at common interpretations of important passages of Scripture as well as encouraging individual hope and faith.

Works of devotional literature also reinforced the sense of legitimacy, authority, and community among nonconformist believers. Bunyan experiences a spiritual awakening after reading Dent's *Plain Man's Pathway to Heaven* (*GA*, 8). He also mentions that Luther's *Commentary on Galatians* reassures him that his experiences are similar to those of other believers at other times (*GA*, 40). The story of Martin Luther's conversion confirms that Bunyan is participating in an experience that is indeed universal and eternal.

The autobiography is written for Bunyan's own spiritual improvement, but it is also written with a specific group of readers in mind. Bunyan writes his account to a congregation of readers who face persecution from nonbelievers as well as temptation from within. His autobiography encourages his readers by describing his success in defeating both types of onslaughts. His audience justifies the positive value of his bad experiences. It also provides a structural model for them to follow in examining and organizing their own experiences. He hopes the documentation of his struggles will encourage his readers to engage in a similar exercise (*GA*, 2). Bunyan wrote *Grace Abounding* to legitimize his authority as a preacher and to strengthen others by providing examples and warnings of the dangers on the path to salvation.

Despite his claims concerning the authority and value of his account, Bunyan's narrative reflects the conflict between his theology and the structural demands of the story. On the one hand, he depicts the search for truth as personal and progressive, the product of an individual effort with a beginning, a middle, and an end. By structuring his account according to the typological reading of the Bible, he creates an expectation that the story will reach a definitive ending with his spiritual redemption. On the other hand, he describes the individual as completely powerless to achieve any level of understanding without divine assistance. He must continually remind himself and his readers that it would be dangerous and even sinful to display any sense of assurance in his salvation. This tension affects how Bunyan tells his story.

Bunyan's word choice and basic grammar reflect the conflict between the demands of the narrative form and his dependence on divine grace. When Bunyan experiences revelations or delusions, he often uses passive verbs, heightening the impression that a battle is being waged over his soul by outside forces.[9] The use of passive verb forms emphasizes Bunyan's helplessness. It counteracts his fears that his entire experience is a product of his own misinterpretations and delusions. If voices and passages of Scripture come from some external source and not from within his own mind, then God or the devil must be interfering directly in his life.

Even when Bunyan does not use the passive voice, he employs other indirect and reflexive forms to emphasize his powerlessness, as well as the sense that he is moving from a limited subjective understanding to a more complete one.[10] When he acknowledges the subjective nature of the apparitions and revelations, he uses phrases like "with the eyes of my understanding" (*GA*, 10) to make the visions seem more external. He thus tries to avoid displaying sinful pride in his own interpretive achievements. Bunyan's word choice reflects his attempts to find a middle ground between affirming the convincing strength of Scripture and affirming his own authority as a preacher and an exegete.

The contradiction between Bunyan's thought and the teleological structure of the narrative has an impact on how he depicts his attempts to read and understand the Bible. Bunyan describes his active engagement — sometimes even his physical struggles — with the text. Nonetheless, he cannot depict himself as having any power in the struggle. Instead, he is dependent on the words interpreting themselves, a struggle between texts and meanings. In order to emphasize his personal impotence in the face of an objective and revealed truth, Bunyan often describes biblical texts as if they are completely external and almost personified. They appear to him as visions or aural delusions, battling each other in the air or running through his mind. His spiritual distress sometimes even warps his perceptions of the physical world (*GA*, 58–59). The more surreal aspects of the text appear because Bunyan combines the theological need to emphasize his own passivity with an attempt to avoid appearing too subjective in the eyes of the reader. He tries to make his mental struggles appear more universal by describing them as physical phenomena and by depicting the battle going on in his mind as a significant episode in the monumental conflict between the forces of good and evil.

Bunyan's autobiography presents certain difficulties in its claim to provide a structural model for a personal narrative. It does trace the accepted path from sin to salvation, but Bunyan is afraid to give it a definite ending. It tries to teach its readers how to understand their experiences, but it is Bunyan's list of temptations rather than his vision of heaven that finally ends the account. These problems involving closure spring from the importance of passivity in Bunyan's concept of grace. To claim to be completely assured of salvation prior to entering heaven would be a sign of pride. By relying on his own certainty, Bunyan would transform himself from the despairing Christian to the arrogant Ignorance. Because dependence on anything but the saving power of Christ's sacrifice is a form of mistaken vanity, Bunyan cannot end his account with a definitive description of the ending of his life story. As long as he lives, the danger to his soul remains. It is always possible that he has made a terrible mistake in interpreting the evidence of his election.

The use of allegory in *The Pilgrim's Progress* neatly avoids the tension present in Bunyan's autobiography between the demands of narrative for a beginning, a middle, and an end, on the one hand, and the spiritual dangers of providing such a conclusion, on the other. Bunyan can write an ending to the story because Christian's victory does not compromise his own struggle for salvation. The move to allegory relieves the tension between structure and theology from the narrator's perspective. As the next chapter will reveal, however, the same conflict reappears in *The Pilgrim's Progress* as a result of the way the text is intended to affect the reader. The story must fulfill the expectations set up by emphasizing the Bible as the source of its structure and function, but it must also teach specific doctrinal lessons for readers to apply to their own lives, including warning them against the danger of complacency. In *The Pilgrim's Progress* Bunyan's gradual movement away from didactic allegory and toward fiction reflects the strength of the Bible as a paradigm not just for the structure of the text but also in terms of its relationship with its readers.

Notes

[1] William Haller, *Foxe's Book of Martyrs and the Elect Nation* (London: Jonathan Cape, 1963), 131.

[2] According to Haller, "What the Bible offered was an imaginative representation of the life of a single people having a unique sense of their identity as a people set apart from all others by a peculiar destiny. It showed a people who thought of the present always as the manifestation of an antecedent design centred upon themselves and certain to be consummated in the proximate future" (53).

[3] John Bunyan, *Grace Abounding to the Chief of Sinners,* ed. Roger Sharrock (Oxford: Clarendon, 1962), 46. Subsequent references to this work are cited in the text using the abbreviation *GA* and page number.

[4] According to N. H. Keeble, "The mode of nonconformist story, that is to say, is at once realistic, allegorical in the old medieval sense, picturing forth theological abstractions, and symbolic in the manner of modern subjectivism, investing particular experiences with figurative significance. Its method was a peculiarly intimate and personal use of the traditional typological exegesis of the Old Testament which survived the Reformation. . . . The details of Old Testament narratives . . . were read as symbolic anticipations of the individual's personal experience and as allegorical representations of the general experience of saints, sinners and nations." *The Literary Culture of Nonconformity in Later Seventeenth-Century England* (Avon, U.K.: Leicester UP, 1987), 264–65.

[5] Martin Luther's influence on Bunyan is visible in the value he attaches to personal spiritual experience. See Richard L. Greaves, *John Bunyan* (Appleford, Berkshire, U.K.: Sutton Courtenay, 1969), 32–33.

[6] He continues to feel the urge to blaspheme in defiance of God even after he has become a preacher. See *GA*, 90.

[7] See W. R. Owens, introduction to *Grace Abounding to the Chief of Sinners*, by John Bunyan, ed. W. R. Owens (Harmondsworth, U.K.: Penguin, 1987), xviii–xix.

[8] Keeble writes that "so complete was the nonconformists' sympathetic identification with biblical texts that they often ceased to express themselves by likening their situation to a biblical precedent and came instead to speak through, and in the words of, such precedents" (251–52).

[9] Here are some examples: "suddenly this conclusion was fastned on my spirit" (*GA*, 10); "though I was thus troubled and tossed and afflicted with the sight and sence and terrour of my own wickedness" (*GA*, 28); "now, how was my Soul led from truth to truth by God!" (*GA*, 37).

[10] Here is a good example: "as still I do remember, presently I found two things within me, at which I did sometimes marvel" (*GA*, 15).

2: Bunyan's *Pilgrim's Progress*

According to John Bunyan, the positive use of words and stories awakens religious belief and strengthens the elect community. In *The Pilgrim's Progress*, part 1 and part 2, he tells the story of his characters' journey through an allegorical landscape, from sin to redemption. Bunyan bases his faith in the transforming power of the story he has created on his faith in the transforming power of the story told in the Bible (*PP*, 4–6). He publishes his work in order to help his readers understand how their actions and attitudes affect their spiritual prospects (*PP*, 6–7). By reading the book, they should be able to learn how to tell their own stories and judge their own moral and spiritual progress.

Bunyan uses other texts to create the landscape through which the pilgrims travel. The allegory combines images from Scripture with the conventions of popular stories of chivalry. The "pilgrimage of life" motif, common in devotional literature of the time, structures the material. Because it is the tale of a journey through a world created by means of words and stories, *The Pilgrim's Progress* is concerned with language and storytelling. Christian, the hero of the first volume, must learn both to understand the signs around him and to tell his own story correctly. His account leads the characters who follow him through their journeys.

The pilgrimage metaphor implies a final destination that is known, albeit obscurely, from the outset of the journey. According to this structure, a right path and a wrong path exist. The traveler's task is to discern the right path, the straight and narrow path of virtue, and to follow it without straying off into sin or temptation. When he follows this preordained path, the pilgrim moves through the world according to scriptural norms and the divine plan.

The characters who travel on a spiritual pilgrimage trace a path through the scriptural narrative. Their final destination — eternal damnation or eternal salvation — is also the ending toward which, according to the Bible, the entire story of mankind leads. Although Bunyan does not provide a map to accompany the text of *The Pilgrim's Progress,* this type of allegory frequently appears in seventeenth-century broadsheet maps illustrating the path of salvation.[1] In Bunyan's text, Great-Heart's map, which shows the ways to the Celestial City, is glossed in the margin as *"God's Book"* (*PP*, 297). The light of Christ illuminates it. Even when it appears in written form, the use of the pilgrimage metaphor presupposes an ethical or moral map based on divine law, whose implied draftsman is God. Scriptural law and scriptural exempla provide the images on which this map is based.

While the theology of the New Testament exerts a clear influence on Bunyan's understanding of grace, proportionally fewer of the images in *The Pilgrim's Progress* are taken from the New Testament (with the exception of the Book of Revelation) than from the Old Testament. Bunyan uses the Old Testament's portrayal of the sufferings and destiny of a chosen people to describe the formation of an elect community as well as to indicate Christian's spiritual progress. Something similar happens in Johann Gottfried Schnabel's *Wunderliche Fata,* where personal stories and the history of the island as a whole are based upon a structure and images derived from the Old Testament. Both authors' interpretations of the Old Testament journey to the Promised Land unite the destiny of the individual with that of the community. Individual protagonists share the experience of physical and spiritual displacement; form a direct relationship with God; follow the Old Testament pattern of temptation, disobedience, and repentance; and emphasize the contrast between the chosen people and the reprobate. Christian, like Albertus Julius, becomes a prophet and a patriarch; his story begins the story of the community of the faithful.

In addition to the central problem of how to interpret subjective experience according to the lessons and examples given in the Bible, *The Pilgrim's Progress* addresses the problem of reconciling passages of Scripture with each other. The relationship of the rule of law in the Old Testament to that of grace in the New Testament is particularly tricky territory for Christian to negotiate. The landscape of the pilgrimage makes tangible Bunyan's attempt to read the canons as a unified narrative.

Faithful's brief story reflects Bunyan's unified reading of the Bible. Faithful describes his individual experience as a movement from the Old to the New Testament, from carnal law to spiritual grace. At the foot of Hill Difficulty Faithful meets Adam the First, who represents original sin and carnal temptation. Adam the First tempts him with sensual lust and pride, but Faithful escapes. Moses, the figure of the Law, then beats him almost senseless for allowing himself to be tempted by the carnal world. Jesus Christ, the embodiment of divine grace, appears to plead for Faithful and enables him to continue on his journey. In this brief relation Faithful demonstrates how his life follows the pattern of the universal *Heilsgeschichte*. Every redeemed individual must experience a similar movement from carnal sin to fear of judgment and from powerless despair to grace and salvation. This movement from the fear of the law to justification through Christ is also the structure of Christian's more detailed story.

The Bible is the major source of the allegorical framework of the pilgrimage because, according to Bunyan, all of human existence is a form of participation in a story created and structured by God. The Bible also appears in various manifestations within the text in order to reveal the dynamic relationship between the book and its readers. Characters read in different ways at different stages of the journey, and different individuals react to the text in different ways. Just as in *Grace Abounding*, the individuals who seek salvation must learn to interpret the Bible in order to understand how to journey through God's story. Its lessons become more detailed, more specific, and more personal as characters progress spiritually.

Bunyan's depiction of the Bible highlights the specific ways in which it affects and defines the life of the individual. The unnamed book that causes Christian's flight is perhaps the most obvious representation of the Bible in *The Pilgrim's Progress*. Christian understands the text only well enough to recognize the difference between the sanctity it recommends and his own, sin-burdened life. Evangelist's guidance shows the importance of help from fellow believers and from God in learning to read and understand Scripture. He distills the teachings of Scripture into a single, practical message and shows Christian where to go (*PP*, 10). As long as Christian reads without help, he remains confused. He understands only enough to know that the people who remain in the City of Destruction are doomed. His faith in Evangelist's interpretation of the Bible is capable of carrying him further than his own reading and interpretive abilities.

In the early stages of his journey the book provides Christian with the words to describe his own spiritual visions. His inability to tell Pliable about the joys of heaven reflects his own incomplete spiritual development (*PP*, 13). Scripture provides a language for spiritual experience. Christian does not progress away from Scripture as he learns to speak with more assurance. Instead, he develops his ability to use and recombine the words of the Bible to describe his own visions to his audience. The final goal of the journey is the state Christian reaches in the Celestial City, where his experience of salvation matches the joys of heaven as foretold in Scripture and everyone speaks by quoting from the Bible.

During his journey Christian tries to develop his ability to retell the lessons of Scripture in a personal way. He must develop a complete understanding of scriptural language and of his own nature according to this language. The better he understands the words of the Bible, the better he will understand himself. The looking glass requested by Mercy in the second volume expresses this relation. Glossed as *"the Word of God"* (*PP*, 287), it enables characters to see themselves correctly. At the same time, it displays all of the detail of Christ's visage. The vision the mirror reveals is always applicable to the individual's situation. These variations reflect the Bible's universal nature. There is something in the mirror to match every aspect of human experience. Despite the variety of lessons, its central meaning is always the same: Christ.

The roll given to Christian as a token of personal election reflects his ability to apply the general promises of Scripture specifically to his individual case. This text represents a more personal, experiential interaction with the Bible than the general warnings given by the book it replaces. Because he is a member of the elect, Scripture is full of passages that have a particular significance for him. When Christian travels alone, reading in the roll replaces conversation with his companions. Its ability to refresh him physically is an indication of the power, truth, and authority of the text. Forgetting the roll shows that he is relying on himself rather than on the tokens and teachings provided by God. Like Ignorance, Christian falls into the trap of arrogant self-sufficiency when he forgets the importance of Scripture in guiding his subjective experience.

The Bible appears in various guises throughout the work, most frequently as a map, like Great-Heart's map in the second volume, or as a note of warning or direction, like the one the shepherds give to Hopeful and Christian. These notes and maps teach Christian to heed specific directions from the text and to follow its signs and warnings. Evangelist also demonstrates the prophetic nature of the Bible when he applies the lessons found in the Bible to foretell Christian's and Faithful's difficulties during the Vanity Fair episode (*PP*, 87). Because personal experience follows the path laid down by Scripture, the pilgrims can anticipate that they will be sorely tested before they are permitted entry into the Promised Land. God tested the faith of the Israelites; like their predecessors, the pilgrims must have confidence that they will be granted a final reward.

A final manifestation of the Bible appears in the letter that Christiana receives at the beginning of the second volume. Like Christian's roll, it shows that Christiana understands that the Bible urges her personally to seek salvation. Reading the Bible transforms her understanding of herself and of the world around her. Christiana's entry into the allegorical landscape of the pilgrimage reflects this transformation. The letter guarantees Christiana's admission at the Wicket Gate, and it provides her with encouragement and refreshment on her journey. It is not, however, a certificate of election. Mercy does not have one, but she is still allowed to pass through the gate. Instead, the letter demonstrates Christiana's receptive reading of the divine text. Christian's example opens the door for her own reading; her relationship with him gives her the courage to believe the Bible's promises. The beginnings of Bunyan's community of the faithful appear in this manifestation of the Bible.

Because the landscape through which Christian and his family travel is founded on the scriptural narrative, its substance is, in essence, linguistic; questions concerning language, both human and divine, pervade the text. Leaving the City of Destruction is leaving behind a world without meaning in order to participate in a world full of meaning. When the pilgrims accept that God is telling a story and that they have a role to play within that story, they also accept the need to read all of the signs around them in order to understand how to take up their assigned roles. As in *Grace Abounding,* Bunyan provides examples of mistaken interpretation and sinful misunderstanding in order to warn his readers against complacency. He contrasts worldly language with the language of the faithful. He uses examples of godly and reprobate language to show how slippery interpretations can be: pride and arrogance define the language of the reprobate, while humility and mutual respect define the language of the redeemed.

There is a clear contrast between the language of the community of the faithful and that of worldly society during the opening scenes of part 1, but the difference appears most clearly during the Vanity Fair episode. When Christian and Faithful reach the fair, their speech is conspicuous:

> For few could understand what they said; they naturally spoke the Language of *Canaan;* But they that kept the *fair,* were the men of this World: So that from one end of the *fair* to the other, they seemed *Barbarians* each to the other. (*PP,* 90)

Their grave words[2] are absolutely intolerable to the populace of the fair, whose words are chaotic, disjointed, and abusive (*PP,* 90). Christian and

Faithful behave with restraint and return ill-treatment with kindness (*PP*, 91). They demonstrate similar social behavior and a consensus in their reactions to others.

In contrast, the inhabitants of Vanity Fair present a vision of human society as Babel. They quarrel among themselves. The men's example moves some and not others. They recognize no common rules for behavior and display no social consensus. In the trial itself witnesses repeat and misinterpret Faithful's words. The witnesses and judges completely lack a context for understanding what he says. Like Christian's neighbors at the beginning of part 1, they do not understand Scripture. It is only after Faithful's death that it appears that some people have understood his example despite all the confusion. There is no conflict between his words and actions; his conduct proves the sincerity of his ideas and the strength of his conviction. His example thus results in Hopeful's conversion, with the assurance that more of the men of the fair will follow. Godly discourse works to build a community, while chaos and destruction are the products of the dissonant, fragmented discourse of the world.

Bunyan uses the Enchanted Ground in order to emphasize the practical differences between the conversation of the godly and the reprobate. In part 1 Christian and Hopeful successfully avoid the threat of sleepiness in the Enchanted Ground by discussing Hopeful's conversion. They keep their minds awake in the present by remembering past difficulties and successes. The conversation is systematic and reasoned. It conforms to the usual pattern of the conversion narrative and retraces Hopeful's mental processes in chronological order. Christian's questions assist Hopeful in organizing his account, just as the interviews with others help Christian to evaluate his past. While Hopeful's story is presented as a positive example, that of Ignorance appears as a negative example. Christian and Hopeful analyze his mistakes as a warning to the faithful. Their complementary knowledge strengthens their interpretations, as when, for example, Hopeful outlines the reasons for backsliding and Christian the manner in which it occurs.

In contrast, in part 2 the pilgrims observe two men who have fallen asleep on the Enchanted Ground. When they are shaken, Heedless and Too Bold each carry on a one-sided conversation. Their words are all in the future tense and they are not organized in a logical or systematic way. What they say is not governed by faith or reason (*PP*, 298). It lacks any connection with the men's past or present experience. The inaction of the speakers contradicts their promises and reveals their hypocrisy. Because learning to tell their stories is such an important part of the pilgrims' journey, flaws like the lack of coherence in their conversation (*PP*, 298) are grave signs of their inability to progress along the path to salvation.

Because of the nature of Bunyan's allegory, the reprobate characters whom Christian meets along the road tend to be examples of bad or rival discourses. Those who are bad in action (like Simple, Sloth, and Presumption) physically leave the path — they are visibly bad — while those whose language is somehow corrupt still *appear* as though they are pious and on pilgrimage. Their hypocrisy and their lack of self-awareness is more threatening to Christian than the temptation to leave the path. His task is to read the discourses of those he comes across properly and to decide whether they are suitable companions for his journey.

By representing the various types of reprobate conversation, Bunyan demonstrates the many different and often subtle varieties of danger and temptation that a believer might encounter. If the process depicted in *The Pilgrim's Progress* is a movement from earthly experience to experience of the scriptural Word, then Talkative's sin is a lack of experimental knowledge of Christian behavior. Faithful and, indeed, the book's readers do not initially perceive the falsity in his ready words, although readers may notice a possible flaw when they hear his frantic listmaking and his name. It is only when Christian makes known the promiscuous nature of his conversation and its hypocrisy — "This man is for any company, and for any *talk*" (*PP*, 78) — that Faithful looks more closely at his words. This reveals the impersonal nature of his speech. Talkative speaks in general platitudes. None of them are heretical, but they do not spring from any personal, felt truth. Because his words are not backed up by experience, Talkative is not confident in his misinterpretations when he is challenged. He shows he is conscious of his hypocrisy by blushing.[3]

On the basis of the encounter with Talkative, Faithful describes the importance of a relationship with God that is experiential and not merely theoretical:

> *Knowledge that resteth in the bare speculation of things, and knowledge that is accompanied with the grace of faith and love, which puts man upon doing even the will of God from the heart: the first of these will serve the Talker, but without the other the true Christian is not content.* (*PP*, 82)

To put the matter rather harshly, only the true Christian is able to speak a language in which meaning and sign, experience and word are connected. True understanding is practical and is based on the personal experience of conversion. Interpreting the Bible and thinking about theology should teach the individual to do the will of God.

The episode involving By-ends, Money-love, Hold-the-World, and Save-all is in many ways similar to the Talkative episode. By-ends uses language and bad company to justify what he knows to be wrongful conduct. These characters relativize language and religion more explicitly than Talkative. They try to justify situations in which religious belief is not an end in itself but rather a means to an end, as though worldly riches might lie beyond the Celestial City. Their use of a sermon or tractlike format of argument in the debate with Hopeful may be designed to echo debates between opportunist Anglicans and the stricter nonconformists in Bunyan's own time.[4] The manipulation of this form illustrates the elasticity of the argument. Their language is so slippery because it is not grounded in any concrete textual or practical example.

The encounter with Ignorance condemns the opposite tendency. His confidence mirrors the interior assurance and the perfectionist doctrine of the early Quakers.[5] Ignorance relies on personal experience without paying attention to the meaning of Scripture or the structure of the religious narrative. Ignorance is damned not because of an extreme reliance on his own perceptive abilities (this is Atheist's sin) but because of a lack of awareness of himself. He fails to recognize his own insufficient and fallible nature. Although he believes in justification by Christ, he fails to feel himself convicted by his own sinfulness. He does not fear divine judgment. Because of this, he does not experience the feelings of helplessness and despair that are the necessary precursors to conversion. He defines the criteria for his salvation according to the prompting of his own heart rather than by listening to others' experiences or by trying to read and understand the Bible. Bunyan uses Ignorance to argue that the stages of the conversion narrative are objectively ordained and necessary for salvation.

Ignorance's failure to tell his story properly demonstrates how important it is for Christian to learn to understand and discuss his experiences correctly. There are two stages in this process. He must first recall and then retell his experiences, organizing and giving them meaning according to whether they assist or hamper his progress toward the Celestial City. The more accurately and truthfully Christian learns to tell the story of his life, the closer he comes to the redemption he seeks.

A series of interviews appears during the early stages of Christian's journey. These interviews emphasize the necessity of learning to tell stories correctly as well as learning to read. Christian's success in answering his examiners' questions reflects his increasing ability to understand his life as a part of the story written and structured by God. Although the questions asked in the interviews sometimes hint at a specific reply, Christian is generally left to relate his story without assistance and is rewarded for correct answers. His increased understanding of the direction in which God is leading him illustrates the benefits of properly interpreting the past as a means of understanding the future. At the end of the examination scenes, his examiners provide warnings and directions for the next portion of his journey.

Benevolent characters ask Christian questions about his experiences no less than eleven times in *The Pilgrim's Progress*.[6] The interviews by Good Will, Interpreter, Porter Watchful, Discretion, and the shepherds all begin with questions about who he is, where he has come from, and where he is going (*PP*, 25). The repetition of the formula at various stages of the journey shows the steadiness of Christian's purpose. He repeats the story of how he changed his name from *Graceless* to *Christian* to demonstrate how radically his decision to set out on pilgrimage has redefined his identity. The repeated formula also measures the progress Christian has made at each stage of his journey. As he becomes more competent in his interpretation, he represents past dangers and mistakes in a slightly different fashion at each interview. He explicitly describes following Worldly-Wiseman as sinful when he relates the story a second time, after Evangelist has rescued him and helped him to understand his danger. This process culminates when Piety leads Christian to select the most significant providences from his story in the House Beautiful.[7] The house is an allegory for the church congregation, and the location reflects the structured, catechistic nature of the exercise.

The examiners also encourage Christian to observe and learn from the conduct of others. For example, Good Will asks him to judge the actions of Obstinate and Pliable. They show Christian — and, through him, the reader — the importance of learning even from experience that is banal or negative. Good Will also discusses the dangers of Mount Sinai with Christian. The fear of the law has caused many deaths (*PP*, 27). The mistakes Christian makes are common mistakes. It is therefore important for individual believers to learn from other people's experiences as well as from their own.

In addition to understanding the significance of his own experiences, Christian must learn to interpret the moral meaning of emblems, signs, and symbols. The episode at the Interpreter's House is another catechistic exercise. Like the examiners, the Interpreter uses a dialogue in the form of questions and answers to instruct the people who view his emblems. The conversation is a favorite among critics of *The Pilgrim's Progress,* many of whom argue that a sense of progression in the emblems accompanies Christian's increasing skills at understanding and interpreting.

The Interpreter schools Christian in the methods of interpreting different kinds of moral examples. Christian needs to learn how to read books and interpret pictures, but he should also be able to understand how other people's experiences might have a moral too. The first emblem, the picture of the visage of Christ, governs all of the interpretations, just as, according to the Interpreter, it must govern every step of Christian's journey. The four short, exemplary plays are general moral emblems. Through them the Interpreter teaches Christian how to understand exemplary events, as well as explaining the direct, moral lessons that each example provides. Christian's discussion with the fifth object for interpretation, the man in the iron cage, teaches him how to learn a lesson from someone else's experience. The iron cage shows him the effect of the man's despair on his moral and spiritual situation. The vision provides a specific warning to Christian, who is always prone to doubt and despair. He questions the man directly and learns to understand the flaws in his thinking through the latter's answers to his questions. The episode is a watershed in the narrative. It is the moment when Christian has acquired enough knowledge, confidence, and authority to move from being questioned to being the questioner.

The early stages of Christian's journey reflect the darkness and isolation of the social outcast, whereas reprobate characters tend to appear in groups.[8] Christian's isolation emphasizes the opposition between the state-sanctioned religion of the masses, a religion of appearance and superficial conformity, on the one hand, and the sincere and, in Bunyan's view, authentic belief of the select nonconformist congregation or individual seeker, on the other. Motivated by the necessity of seeking his salvation, Christian, unlike many of the characters in the other novels, *voluntarily* chooses his isolation. Bunyan does not, however, depict solitude as a desirable state. Christian must leave his family and neighbors in order to save his own soul, but only after he has been unsuccessful in his bid for company on the journey. The wrench of this displacement becomes a feature in the retelling of his story, particularly in part 2, when Christian's departure appears as the beginning of the story of the conversion of his wife and children.

As was the case in *Grace Abounding*, conversation with fellow believers is very important to Bunyan as a way of verifying personal interpretations of experience and Scripture. Bunyan consistently condemns unchecked subjectivity and self-reliance. During the solitary portions of his journey, Christian overcomes his isolation by talking and reading to himself (*PP*, 41). He tries to transcend his spiritual isolation by creating a dialogue between several voices, just like Robinson Crusoe does on his island.

Christian's goal is to learn to speak to himself authoritatively through the voice of Scripture. To better understand how this works in terms of allegory, a real-life example is helpful. A friend was eating a sandwich. As she dropped bits of it on the table, speaking in her mother's voice she said, "Get a plate, Muriel!" For a second she split herself in two. Muriel addressed her naïve, childlike self at the same time as she spoke with the voice of adult authority, telling herself what to do in order to behave well. The aim of Christian's reading of the Bible is to internalize God's voice in the same way that most people internalize the voices of their parents. The voice of Scripture will tell him what to do even when he is most mistaken or confused. The relative peacefulness and calm of his conversations with himself indicate that Christian has moved beyond his desperate, incoherent, undirected cries at the beginning of the text (*PP*, 8) and toward a structured and organized discourse. Internalizing the voice of Scripture stabilizes his interactions with himself.

Bunyan describes Christian's interactions with Faithful and Hopeful in order to illustrate the specific benefits of conversation with fellow believers. Christian hears Faithful singing the twenty-third psalm in the Valley of the Shadow of Death. Because Faithful uses the words of the Bible, he appears as a friend and not as a threat. Like Christian, he tells himself what to do and how to understand his surroundings by using quotations from Scripture. God is guiding him, and his words are the words of the comforted. By comparing his own situation with Faithful's, Christian realizes that comfort will come to him too. Faithful's presence corrects Christian's mistaken perceptions and his temporary lack of faith in God's guidance. His singing shows Christian that he is not the only one undergoing a trial. It encourages Christian to believe that God is with them both and redirects his attention forward because he hopes for company (*PP*, 64). It is no accident that morning arrives shortly after Christian hears the voice. It is only with Faithful's assistance that he is able to overcome the blindness of his despair through the two valleys.

Throughout the text Bunyan shows the value of pious conversation in furthering spiritual growth. When Hopeful tells Christian his story, he is confirming that his understanding of his experiences is correct by telling them to a receptive and judgmental listener. Sharing life stories provides reassurance concerning the universal nature of certain religious experiences (for example, the stages of conversion). Hopeful's ability to organize his story into lists emphasizes its structure. He has gained control over his sinful activities and confused states of mind by learning to sort them out and organize them in a way that makes their meaning clearer in terms of the entirety of his experience. Ignorance's story follows Hopeful's account. It does not display the same degree of structure and organization. It lacks some of the important stages that Hopeful's narrative contains, particularly the moment of despair and the conviction of sin. The comparison with Hopeful's and Christian's stories makes the flaws in Ignorance's story more obvious.

These contrasting examples show how important it is for believers to share and compare their stories in order to make sure they are not incomplete or heretical. Ignorance's negative attitude toward the fellowship of believers is a sign of his reprobate nature. He errs by relying on his own certainty of election rather than on any assurance received from God. He also refuses to listen to Christian's and Hopeful's concerns about his lack of self-awareness. Ignorance will only accept company that reconfirms his own view of himself. When it emerges that he has not had the same experiences as Christian and Hopeful — they have received revelations, with Christ as their guarantor — Ignorance's equivocal answer and his refusal to accept this truth is particularly damning (*PP*, 149). He is simply not interested in telling his story to others, nor does he recognize the value of exchanging and evaluating stories in providing spiritual assistance or confirming his election.

As members of the elect community, Christian and his companions also use social consensus to avoid danger. The Giant Despair episode occurs because the pilgrims fail to realize that they have equal spiritual authority even though Christian is older. Hopeful is ready to follow Christian's guidance even if the latter's ideas conflict with what Hopeful believes is correct. He errs by curbing his tongue. He thus contravenes the principle of plain speech and sincerity that is the essence of Bunyan's recommendation for true Christianity. The pilgrims must come to a consensus in their understanding of the world around them. Scriptural examples and norms, not the carnal, social hierarchy, must form the basis of this understanding.

Christian does speak with authority when he tells the story of Little Faith. He corrects Hopeful's misunderstanding of the tale by comparing it with biblical precedents. He is successful in this case because his interpretations agree with models from the Bible. He can also apply the lessons of the story to Hopeful's own life. This communal process of narrating, listening, and learning to understand stories is the central aspect of the mutual support afforded by companionship during the journey toward salvation.

The role of storytelling in fostering a sense of community becomes increasingly important in part 2. Social interaction is central to the more gentle journey described in the text. Because part 2 is the story of an entire congregation of travelers who share a common language from the beginning of their journey, the sense of isolation and threat to the individual pilgrim disappears. The numbers in the group and the presence of a guide dispel the danger posed by rival discourses or mistaken interpretations.

The greater emphasis on the social interaction of characters in part 2 highlights the role of storytelling in creating an emotional bond between the receptive listener and the narrator. The listener's response to a story occurs on an emotional level as well as on a rational level. Feelings are important because of the role of despair and redemption in Bunyan's understanding of the conversion experience. The community is unified because the individuals within it experience common emotions during their search for salvation. They use similar words and terminology to describe these emotional experiences. When Christiana responds sympathetically to Christian's story, she demonstrates that she shares the same criteria for understanding his experiences. Her past experience and her understanding of Scripture lead her to interpret the story in the same way as the narrator.

Bunyan uses Christiana's departure at the beginning of part 2 to illustrate the difference between unsympathetic and sympathetic listeners. The circle of gossips that condemns Christiana acts as an anti-congregation to the spiritual community that appears in the course of the story. They strengthen vice in each other through evil report rather than using communication constructively to encourage virtue. Christiana's views appear as a form of madness to Mrs. Timorous and her companions (*PP*, 182–83). They simply cannot understand her. Mrs. Inconsiderate makes her lack of sympathy for Christiana quite clear:

> Should she stay where she dwels, and retain this her mind, who could live quietly by her? for she will either be dumpish or un-neighbourly, or talk of such matters as no wise body can abide: Wherefore, for my part,

> I shall never be sorry for her departure; let her go, and let better come in her room: 'twas never a good World since these whimsical Fools dwelt in it. (*PP*, 185)

Worldly society cannot accommodate itself to virtuous people because they base their words upon the language and teachings of Scripture. Christiana's speech implicitly condemns the carnal loyalties of her neighbors. They know that they act in a way that is contrary to the lessons taught by her religion; they do not possess a shared set of values or even a common vocabulary. The total rejection of her language and her story by her intolerant neighbors isolates Christiana completely.

Christiana's central regret is her failure to listen to her husband. Her unsympathetic listening has destroyed her marriage bond. Her sense of guilt focuses on her hard heart (*PP*, 177). When she decides to set off on her own journey, she becomes a sympathetic listener to her husband's story. In doing this, she overcomes the rift between them. Mercy decides to accompany Christiana because of her emotional attachment to her friend and her sympathetic listening to Christiana's words. What Mercy hears during her visit to Christiana's house awakens her desire for further communication. What attracts her about Christiana's words is their truth and their *life* (*PP*, 183). The meaning of the Bible manifests itself in the lives of individuals. When Christiana tells her story using scriptural norms and images, she demonstrates that the Bible is a narrative that is actively present in the past and the future of each experiencing individual. Her story becomes more compelling because it is told as an element of a more universal story. That story has its own power to convince its reader of its truth and authority. Telling stories is a continuous process, a living within the Bible as it endlessly unfolds itself in individual lives.

In part 2 Bunyan describes the possible variations of positive spiritual experience. These variations on Christian's previous, paradigmatic experiences show which aspects of the spiritual life story are necessary and universal and which are different for different people. Mercy, like the other pilgrims the family meets along the way, represents some of these possible variations. Unlike Christian, who is an example for every reader, Bunyan describes Mercy as an example for young girls. Her interactions with Christiana appear more realistic than those between Christian and his almost interchangeable companions Faithful and Hopeful, because of the differences between the experiences of the matron and her young companion. Mercy's narrative does not follow the pattern of Christiana's. She has received no letter of welcome and has had no portentous dreams. She decides to follow Christiana solely because of the attractiveness of the latter's message and her sympathy for Christiana as a friend. Nonetheless, Mercy is accepted at the Wicket Gate. The Interpreter reassures Mercy that her spiritual experience and her election are no less legitimate even though she has not received divine revelations or a specific call.

The episode clarifies the role of virtuous companionship along the journey. Christiana is responsible for encouraging her friend to accompany her despite the lack of an invitation. Her efforts to intercede on Mercy's behalf at the gate, although well-intentioned, remain ineffective. Mercy has to knock for herself and trust in the grace of Christ. Entry into the company of the elect occurs only on an individual basis. Characters can assist and encourage each other during the stages of the journey through which each person must pass (for example, the Wicket Gate and the River of Death). When strengthened by the virtuous and sympathetic exchange of stories, the connections of love, blood, and marriage can modify subjective perceptions, prevent ignorant mistakes, and encourage personal merit, as Christian's example does for Christiana. They are, however, unable to influence those aspects of the pilgrimage — namely, election and reprobation — that depend on the divine rather than the human will. The social community remains subservient both to the structuring principles of doctrine and to the master narrative through which individuals travel.

When Christiana's group of pilgrims reach the Land of Beulah at the end of part 2, they do not sleep, nor do they experience the spontaneous, unconscious speech that Christian and Hopeful experience. Bunyan's description of the Land of Beulah demonstrates the ideal qualities of the language of the blessed. The pilgrims cannot sleep because of the sound of bells and trumpets, and the continuous, joyful reports of the inhabitants. Instead of the individual revelation granted to the pilgrims in part 1, shared narrative is the focus of this earthly paradise. These pilgrims tell their own stories. They also participate in the reports of others as listeners. They hear current narratives as well as the stories of the pilgrims of old.

During the rest in Beulah, the specific identities of the pilgrims disappear for a time. Bunyan refers to them collectively in company with the other nameless inhabitants of the land. They only regain their specific names when summoned to cross the River of Death. The namelessness emphasizes the common elements and universal nature of the discourse in this land. These individuals are not so much the originators of a personal story as the recipients of a universal story that includes them all. Beulah's inhabitants possess a shared set of referents, and all partake of the true Word. Individual definitions and meanings no longer exist; the identities of the individual narrators of the story are of less importance than the fact that they are telling a bit of the same all-encompassing story.

According to Bunyan, the earthly community of the elect provides a foretaste of the heavenly communion of saints. He depicts this earthly community, based on the mutual exchange of life stories, as a positive alternative to the alienation felt by the virtuous individual traveling through a sinful world. As an individual narrative, the story of each character becomes just one among an infinite number of component stories of the scriptural narrative, which is the story and, in Mercy's words, the life of all creation. By extension, through the pilgrims' example actual readers of the text are encouraged to understand their own stories according to the same paradigm. Bunyan's vision of the righteous community and the regenerate world is a vision of a narrative paradise, structured and sustained by an endless narrative exchange, a manifold generation and regeneration of the single, universal story written by a divine author.

The purpose of *The Pilgrim's Progress* is to transform the lives of its readers. This transformation occurs in two ways. The first way of reading the text is practical. It involves applying the specific lessons of the text to the reader's personal life. The reader uses the work like a sermon, learning how to make moral and doctrinal judgments from the examples in the book. The second way closes the gap between the reader and the text. By participating vicariously and sympathetically in the experiences of the individual pilgrims, the reader becomes caught up in the text. Entering the allegory leads the reader to follow the path of its source text — the Bible — and this experience completely transfigures his or her life. Motivated by their sympathetic association with Christian, readers themselves set out on the journey toward salvation by joining the community of pilgrims. With the help of the allegory, they move from their sinful, secular lives to enter a new territory based on scriptural norms and the story told by the Bible.

The sense of involvement by the reader in the text begins in the first pages of Bunyan's allegory. The dreamer narrates the work as it has been revealed to him; he often speaks as if he were reading Christian's journey. During the conversation between the dreamer and Mr. Sagacity in part 2, the dreamer hints at the exemplary purpose of the narrative. He hopes that the report may affect his readers enough to impel them to follow Christian's example (*PP*, 176). To open the book is to enter a community of narrators and readers, all of whose words are based upon their shared understanding of the authority of a common text.

By virtue of the reading process, the storytelling within the text expands to include the actual reader, whom the narrator encourages to accompany Christian on the journey through the allegorical landscape. The readerly nature of the dreamer's interaction with the text appears in his tendency to follow and observe rather than to anticipate and foreshadow the actions of the protagonist. Phrases like "I looked" and "I saw" appear throughout the work. These remind the actual reader that Christian's text is being read at the very moment his actions take place. The phrases return the reader from a state of vicarious participation in the text to being conscious of the text as a book, a work with a central didactic purpose that requires study and interpretation.

The biblical narrative plays a more complex role as a source of the often inconsistent allegorical framework of the story than as a clearly defined symbol within the text. Christian's journey is a journey through narrative, through the land of Scripture. The very scriptural quotations that seem to assail Bunyan's senses in his autobiography are here even more physically present as landmarks and topographical features. When Lot's wife, the pillar of salt, appears as a concrete, empirical example to Christian and Hopeful (*PP*, 108), their failure to heed her warning also becomes an example of how the reader should not read the Bible. The text emphasizes the important moral lessons biblical stories teach, but it also becomes an example in and of itself by showing the reader how to react to these biblical tales.

Christiana's journey through the scriptural landscape previously experienced by her husband adds a further level of complexity to the narrative. The allegory in part 2 has two main source texts, part 1 and the Bible. The way characters in part 2 treat part 1 demonstrates the practical similarities between how reading the Bible and reading part 1 are supposed to affect the reader. Both motivate their readers to set out on a pilgrimage. Both provide images and metaphors by which to judge and understand personal experience. When the characters in part 2 visit the locations of events in part 1, they find that Christian's story has changed their journey. His example has helped to convert Vanity Fair and to fence off the bypaths of Hill Difficulty. Plaques and monuments commemorate his experiences and warn travelers along the same route. The references to part 1 emphasize the exemplary value of the first text to the characters in the second book as well as to the reader.

There are specific lessons to be derived from the two works. Reprobate characters warn against particular sins. Readers can discern their own election by comparing themselves with the characters in the text. By heeding the warnings they represent, readers may avoid making their mistakes (*PP*, 6–7). Features in the landscape represent spiritual dangers, making them easy to remember. Bunyan encourages readers to use Christian's story as a mnemonic aid.[9] As with the Bible, reading *The Pilgrim's Progress* should trigger a process of active interpretation and personal reflection. Readers should try to apply the lessons Christian learns to their own experiences. Christian's story serves as a model to help them organize and understand the various stages in their own spiritual journeys. Bunyan intends *The Pilgrim's Progress* to function in much the same way as the scheme that Piety gives to Christiana in part 2: "Upon which thou mayest look when thou findest thy self forgetful, and call those things again to remembrance for thy Edification, and comfort" (*PP*, 236). It is a vehicle by means of which readers can learn to read and remember their own autobiographical stories.

The prologues to the two volumes of *The Pilgrim's Progress* outline the book's intended didactic function. The work calls for a more active intellectual involvement by the reader than most fictional works, but it is still written in the form of a story and not that of a religious tract or self-help manual. There is therefore always a certain tension between the reader's emotional association with the characters and the serious didactic aspect of the text. On the one hand, Christiana's example indicates that Bunyan intends the reader to follow Christian's physical journey vicariously and emotionally. On the other hand, the dreamer frequently draws attention to the processes of reading and narrating the story and to the links between elements of this story and those of the Bible. He urges the reader to stay awake intellectually and to interpret this text consciously as a fictional construct.

In his introduction to part 1 Bunyan makes it clear that his readers are not *only* supposed to read intellectually and reflectively. The text exercises a good influence on its readers in part because it is original, entertaining, and pleasant to read (*PP*, 7). In order to transfigure the reader, the reading process must also be emotional.[10] According to the prologue in part 2 the strength of the reader's emotional association with exemplary characters correspondingly strengthens the impact of the text. By participating vicariously in the experiences of the positive characters who most resemble themselves, individual readers learn how to confront specific obstacles to their faith. Mercy is an example meant to encourage young maids; the figure of Honest may convert old men (*PP*, 172).

In part 1 Christian's story teaches a set of lessons that aspire to be universal, but in part 2 Bunyan acknowledges the value of strengthening the reader's vicarious participation in the text. He gives his characters more defined personalities and makes them face hardships more specific to their social roles. Fiction tends to eclipse doctrine as his characters transform themselves from moral examples who teach difficult lessons into individuals with satisfactory lives of their own. The movement from allegory to fiction in part 2 parallels Bunyan's increasing emphasis on the moral value of the reader's vicarious participation in the text and the positive effects of sympathetic and affective reading. It also resolves a related problem, namely, the alienation of the reader after Christian enters the Celestial City at the end of part 1.

As an example of third-person narration, Bunyan's work contrasts with the other texts. The stories told by first-person narrators end when the account of the narrator's past catches up with his or her present state. The experiencing and the reflecting self become one and the same. The story ends with a comforting sense of unity. It is not possible for this type of unity to occur at the end of part 1 of *The Pilgrim's Progress*. The story comes to a unified — even happy — ending with Christian's entry into the Celestial City, but it is an ending into which even the dreamer gets only an uncertain peek. The spiritual homeland is not earthly but wholly beyond perception and description. The reader, the commentator, the dreamer, and even the author are left outside the gates with Ignorance.

As long as Christian experiences a certain tension in his attempts to interpret his experiences, readers participate in Christian's journey as a construct of this tension. Because the story of creation that the Bible describes is the story of mankind, each individual story takes place as a part of a more comprehensive narrative that is often difficult to see and to understand. The allegorical images in the text are physical emblems that show both the main character and the reader how his experiences fit into the story that God is telling. When there is no longer a gap between Christian's understanding of his individual story and God's master plan — in other words, when he succeeds in entering God's story completely by recognizing his own role within this more comprehensive narrative — the allegory disappears. The layers of the narrative — the dreamer, the marginal glosses, the implied reader — that focus on interpreting the meaning of Christian's journey are left without any material to interpret. While the narrator and the reader tend to possess a superior perspective compared to Christian's limited understanding during his travels, they cannot reach the level of knowledge he attains when he experiences redemption. The marginal glosses and the dreamer's commentary lose their reconciling impetus because there is nothing left to reconcile. There is no longer a gap between the character's experiences and his ability to understand them correctly.

Christian's story provides an example to pious readers, but once he dies and goes to heaven, his example ceases to apply. Readers cannot participate vicariously in Christian's experience when the latter has become impossible to describe. Christian transcends the narrative by entering the Celestial City, but the reader, along with the dreamer, wakes up in the Den. The reader and the narrator still have to seek their own salvation after they have finished the book. The text ends with Ignorance's damnation, a dire warning concerning the necessity of endless vigilance. It fails to provide any model for maintaining a positive religious state, if such a state is achieved before death.

Ignorance's sorry fate reflects Bunyan's uncertainty — almost paranoia — regarding the impossibility of being completely assured of his election. The reader is not meant to close the book with a feeling of peace and happiness at Christian's salvation. Rather, Ignorance's example should spur readers to further striving. As in Bunyan's autobiography, providing a satisfying and final ending conflicts with the spiritual danger of reaching a state of rest. To participate, even vicariously, in celebrating Christian's assurance of salvation could mean the relaxation of the reader's vigilance in favor of self-satisfaction and complacency. The story's ending is sad because it leaves the reader with such a great sense of abandonment. Almost the only response a reader can make to this ending is to flip back to the beginning and start reading again in hopes of learning from and participating in the text to the extent that he or she *will* be able to enter the Celestial City with Christian. For Christian the story is over. For the reader the story will not end.

The ending of part 2 of *The Pilgrim's Progress* resolves the first part's lack of a satisfactory ending for the reader. Bunyan reads the Bible as a single story with a strong structure and a definite movement toward the ending predicted in the Book of Revelation. He also uses this way of reading the Bible to structure how he organizes and tells life stories. The difference between part 1 and part 2 reflects the impetus toward closure that characterizes the structure of Bunyan's stories. An ending that aspires to be definitive in the same way that the Bible's ending is definitive must be comprehensive. The only way to finish the story in a way that is really unified is to change its focus so that it becomes capable of including all of the participants in the storytelling process. The qualms Bunyan displays in part 1 concerning the dangers of the reader's vicarious participation in Christian's happy ending are supplanted in part 2 by the demands of the story — namely, to provide a beginning, middle, and end for the protagonist, the reader, and even the narrator — which eclipse his previous emphasis on the necessity of ceaseless vigilance in the face of the uncertainty of salvation.

In part 2 the destination of the spiritual journey is not merely transcendent. Unlike the Celestial City, the Land of Beulah is not an area beyond language and description. Instead, it becomes a satisfying home for the book's characters and for its readers. The community of the faithful, living on the banks of the River of Death, anticipates and foreshadows the Celestial City. It gives the story a happy ending because of the sense that the community continues into the future in a harmonious, conflict-free state. Like the narrators in *Springinsfeld, Crusoe,* and the final volume of the *Wunderliche Fata,* the dreamer even mentions the possibility of returning at some point for another visit (*PP,* 311). The faithful still live in the earthly paradise even though the tensions and anxieties that created the plot have subsided. The reader should learn about the necessity of unceasing vigilance and self-examination from part 1. The comfort that part 2 provides is the sense of an ending that is both conclusive and inclusive.

The ending of part 2 is one that the reader can understand and in which he or she can participate because the community of the faithful in the Land of Beulah is created by means of language. Characters enter the community by exchanging stories and interpretations, developing shared definitions, and learning to interpret and understand God's story. According to Bunyan, the Bible is the basis of the reader's actual existence as well as of the characters' fictional existence. The reader participates in the same process of sympathetic listening, interpreting, and developing shared definitions as the characters in the book. The community in the Land of Beulah thus extends beyond the boundaries of the fictional work into the reader's reality. By reading sympathetically and participating vicariously in the characters' journey of interpretation and in their consensus, the reader becomes a part of this same community.

By providing a satisfactory fictional conclusion to the work, Bunyan gives the literary aspect of his biblical structure — the need to provide a satisfactory and universal ending — precedence over the specific doctrinal concerns that characterize the ending of part 1. In the course of the two volumes, the character of the Bible as *the* ultimate story — inclusive, comprehensive, and applicable to every individual — completely eclipses the issue of individual uncertainty. Learning to tell and read stories, speaking the language of the blessed, and entering the community made up of storytellers become surer signs of election than any of the spiritual doubts or tortured misgivings intended to reassure the reader about the narrator's sanctity in *Grace Abounding*.

The final lesson of Bunyan's text is that language creates its own reality. The goal of the storytelling process is to unlock the true, hidden narrative that defines human existence. Stories, not physical objects, are the substance of creation. Readers and characters must become like the man at Mount-Marvel who *"tumbled the Hills about with Words"* (*PP*, 285). If they can come to an understanding of their experiences that agrees with the story that God is telling, they will be able to overcome any obstacle. Christian needs to remember that he holds the key of Promise in his bosom. Like the characters in *The Pilgrim's Progress,* readers must always be aware that the path to salvation lies through a landscape that is not carnal and physical but rather is made of signs and meanings. Reaching the end is entering God's story. Readers find salvation by overcoming the separation between themselves and the text.

As a work that imitates the Bible and mediates between its readers and the Bible, Bunyan's *Pilgrim's Progress* assumes some of the function and authority of Scripture. Although it serves as a vehicle to lead its readers to salvation, by depicting the state of salvation as fictional and social rather than transcendent and spiritual the story affirms its own power and ability to create an alternative reality for its readers. In *The Pilgrim's Progress*, as in *Grace Abounding,* Bunyan describes how communication between believers creates a set of shared meanings and narrative patterns. The source of this intersubjective consensus lies in Scripture, but exchanging stories and interpreting texts takes on a life of its own. The endless unfolding of the Bible's meaning in personal experience, in allegoresis, and in the imagination transcends the letter of Scripture. In moving toward fiction and concentrating on the value of social interaction in creating meaning, Bunyan foreshadows the tendency to use fiction to replace the Bible apparent in the novels of Grimmelshausen, Defoe, and Schnabel.

Truth and life reside in the Bible, but they also appear in the stories that affirm and reveal the Bible as the hidden meaning behind all personal experience, whether these stories are autobiographical or fictional. Bunyan ultimately celebrates narration as a constructive and life-giving force in and of itself. Because the Bible is a story — is *the* story — all good stories partake of its power and authority.

Notes

[1] See Tessa Watt, *Cheap Print and Popular Piety, 1550–1640* (Cambridge: Cambridge UP, 1991), 236.

[2] They will only say: *"We buy the Truth"* (*PP*, 90).

[3] See David J. Alpaugh, "Emblem and Interpretation in *The Pilgrim's Progress*," *ELH* 33 (1966): 306.

[4] See Isabel Rivers, "Grace, Holiness, and the Pursuit of Happiness: Bunyan and Restoration Latitudinarianism," in *John Bunyan: Conventicle and Parnassus, Tercentenary Essays*, ed. N. H. Keeble (Oxford: Clarendon, 1988), 63–67.

[5] See Richard F. Hardin, "Bunyan, Mr. Ignorance, and the Quakers," *Studies in Philology* 69 (1972): 496.

[6] Evangelist (9, 20), Good Will (25), Interpreter (28), Porter Watchful (46), Discretion (46), Piety (47), Prudence (49), Charity (52), Evangelist (86), and the Shepherds (119–20).

[7] See Kathleen M. Swaim, *Pilgrim's Progress, Puritan Progress: Discourses and Contexts* (Chicago: U of Illinois P, 1993), 150.

[8] For example: Simple, Sloth, and Presumption; Formalist and Hypocrisy; Timorous and Mistrust; By-ends, Money-love, and Save-all; and the inhabitants of Vanity Fair.

[9] *"Art thou forgetful? . . . Then read my fancies, they will stick like Burs, / And may be to the Helpless, Comforters"* (*PP*, 7).

[10] *"O then come hither, / And lay my Book, thy Head and Heart together"* (*PP*, 7).

3: Grimmelshausen's *Der Abentheurliche Simplicissimus Teutsch* and *Der seltzame Springinsfeld*

THIS CHAPTER CONSIDERS THE importance of language, storytelling, and the justification of fiction in Grimmelshausen's *Der Abentheurliche Simplicissimus Teutsch* in relation to moral and religious tensions similar to those that appear in Bunyan's texts. Like *The Pilgrim's Progress*, *Simplicissimus* contains many ambiguities and contradictions, but it is possible to arrive at a satisfactory interpretation of the text by taking its moral element into consideration. In order to understand more completely what the book is saying about the value of fiction, this chapter will also examine one of its sequels, *Der seltzame Springinsfeld,* and briefly discuss some of Grimmelshausen's other texts.

In the first chapter of the second volume, the *Continuatio*, Grimmelshausen describes the exemplary and didactic role of *Simplicissimus* while defending it against his critics. He uses the metaphor of the sugar-coated pill to argue that his book exposes folly in order to encourage virtue. Simplicius's stories serve moral aims similar to those that might inform a sermon. His amusing experiences teach readers how not to act; these moral lessons justify the work's publication. Although this sounds very similar to the justification Bunyan uses in his verse prefaces to the two parts of *The Pilgrim's Progress*, there is an important difference in terms of how Grimmelshausen applies the defense to his text. The lessons in Bunyan's text are both moral and spiritual, whereas the lessons in Grimmelshausen's text are almost exclusively moral. Simplicius criticizes sinful behavior, but he does not teach his readers how to improve themselves.

Unlike Bunyan, who creates a spiritual and (eventually) a social alternative to sinful existence, Grimmelshausen does not depict any imitable, positive alternative to the wicked world in *Simplicissimus*. The book is a product of the tension between religious guidelines for moral behavior and the reality of the protagonist's practical experience. Grimmelshausen criticizes negative examples of worldly conduct in order to instruct his readers. He describes a society that is so blinded by sin that biblical paradigms have no power to define characters' actions. His characters seldom realize that their shortsighted attempts to satisfy their physical desires prevent them from understanding the reality or the moral value of their experiences. Simplicius finally comes to understand that people only see what they want to see; their folly deceives them.[1] The lesson the book teaches its readers is the same lesson he learns during his experiences, namely, that constant change characterizes life in the corrupt world.[2]

The world of corrupt experience is too powerful, all-encompassing, and interesting for Simplicius to deny it completely by separating himself from it. During his life he continually tries to create a space on the borders of the world. His story may affirm the necessity — even the value — of worldly experience, but he must also learn from these experiences. Understanding the world does not consist in moving away from the realm of outward appearances to perceive their hidden meanings so much as it does in perceiving both appearance and meaning at the same time. Insofar as he achieves this balance, it becomes visible in the moral gloss Simplicius gives to his story when he comments on his experiences at the end of each chapter. His story is entertaining, amusing, and filled with trickery, but it also uses satire for a moral purpose. By exposing just how corrupt the world is, Simplicius seeks to establish (at the very least) the extent to which it does not follow the religious and moral values that it claims to accept. He can only escape the sinfulness of the world when he learns to recognize the extreme gap between human values and human actions.

What is the source of Simplicius's moral perspective in the novel? Popular devotional literature, which at the time tended to transcend confessional boundaries, influences all of the works discussed in this book. Despite the bitter religious conflicts of the seventeenth century, surveys of publishing lists reveal a surprising overlap between literature of different confessions on the lists of individual printers.[3] In England many radical Protestants read Roman Catholic devotional texts,[4] and Thomas à Kempis's *Imitation of Christ* was a seventeenth-century best seller.[5] Protestant authors read and adapted pictures and poems from Roman Catholic emblem books. Fictional works were another vehicle for interconfessional exchange. Grimmelshausen imitates aspects of Aegidius Albertinus's overtly Catholic translation of *Guzmán de Alfarache* (Guzman of Alfaraque, 1615),[6] but picaresque novels also exert a strong influence on Defoe and Schnabel. As a child John Bunyan read chapbook versions of medieval folktales and popular romances like *The Seven Champions of Christendom*.[7]

All of the works under discussion have an interconfessional element. The special emphasis on the community of believers in Schnabel's *Wunderliche Fata* reflects the dual influence of Lutheran and puritan belief on the pietist movement. Nonconformists like Bunyan and Defoe defined themselves as members of a line of dissent stretching back through the first Lutherans and Wycliffe to the early church. Bunyan reads Luther, while the Roman Catholics in *Robinson Crusoe* defy the hero's expectations by dealing with him fairly and honestly. Simplicius makes positive comments about the Hutterites and forms friendships with Lutheran ministers and a Reformed pastor even though, like Grimmelshausen himself, he ends up a Roman Catholic.

The content of the book rather than the specific creed of the author justifies the merit of devotional works in the early modern period. All of the books under discussion follow the model of devotional literature by recommending a similar general, inoffensive set of moral guidelines: obey the Ten Commandments; avoid the sins of the flesh and those of the spirit. Unlike argumentative texts and religious propaganda, devotional works tend to avoid specific dogmatic arguments while emphasizing personal spiritual development and morality. The fictional works discussed in this book share the same tendency. While critics speculate that some of Bunyan's reprobate characters may represent members of other confessions, their names simply describe their psychological failings. Regardless of confession, any believer could fall into similar errors of thought. Schnabel presents Roman Catholics as examples of the most corrupt personal morality, but he never describes any theological reasons for his prejudice. He still allows a Spaniard, Don Cyrillo de Valaro, to play a central role in the founding of the Felsenburg civilization. During Tischler Lademann's story, he acknowledges that even a Roman Catholic bishop might possibly adhere to a decent and honest moral code.

While the explicitly religious aspects of the texts under discussion focus on general Christian morality and personal spiritual development, variations in the understanding of original sin and the operation of divine grace do affect the plots of these works. Bunyan and Defoe emphasize the necessity of the experience of Christ's imputed righteousness to justify the believer, while Schnabel stresses the importance of passive despair as a precursor to conversion. Bunyan, Defoe, and Schnabel appear to follow Martin Luther's idea that the individual search for salvation is an attempt to regain the near-perfect nature of prelapsarian man. God gave Adam physical perfection, a mastery over creation, great knowledge, and good judgment.[8] Individuals must measure their failings against this standard.[9] The purpose of the spiritual journey is to regain these qualities by returning to a state of harmony with God.

Luther develops his belief that man must seek a return to his natural, prelapsarian state (*natura integra*) from Saint Augustine.[10] The latter links his concept of human life as a process of returning to God with his understanding of memory and, through memory, with his understanding of the function of autobiography. Augustinian ideas about memory appear in such influential seventeenth-century writings as Johann Arndt's *Vier Bücher vom Wahren Christenthum* (Four Books Concerning True Christianity, 1606–10) and form the core structure of the Protestant works. For Augustine memory is the force that impels creation to return consciously to participation in its Source. Gaining knowledge helps man to return to acting in harmony with God. The more he learns and understands, the better he can approach his prelapsarian state. The individual life story recreates past experiences, but the narrator's more informed, less ignorant perspective allows him to understand how these experiences — even the negative ones — fit into a greater whole. God uses human experience to reveal a single, grand story. When the enlightened narrator finishes telling his story, he has come to an understanding not only of the role God plays in his own life but of the way his individual return to God is synonymous with the relationship between God and the whole of creation. Creation is the spelling out of a divine story. By understanding and telling this same story the individual narrator learns to act in the image of God.

There are two important points to be aware of in this context. First, the Protestant narrators learn to tell their stories by understanding the relationship between their own experiences and God's master narrative. Once they come to understand the way God interferes in their lives and learn to read where he is leading them through their experiences, they are able to act in harmony with God's intentions. They reverse the damaging effects of the Fall by regaining their Adamic perfection. Second, the structure of the life stories in the Protestant works loosely follows the basic structure of the *Confessions* by depicting the return to God as a gradual process. Even though these works emphasize the theology of divine grace and the helplessness of the predestined individual, their protagonists are actually very active. They learn to interpret their surroundings in a way that is more or less cumulative.

While there is always room for error, on the whole the stories describe how characters learn from their mistakes and build on their successes.

Whereas Roman Catholics believe in the efficacy of works, Protestants do not. Nevertheless, the plot structure of the Protestant books seems to indicate that it is possible for a character to work toward salvation even if it contradicts the authors' theoretical beliefs in the role of divine grace. To counteract his linear plot Bunyan constantly has to remind his readers that his characters can fail at any stage in their journey. Defoe gets around the same hurdle by focusing on the development of Crusoe's reason more than on his religious thought. Like any other form of education, learning to think rationally tends to be cumulative. If God works in ways that are inherently reasonable, it seems natural that the search for salvation should proceed in a more or less linear fashion. The sense of progression in Schnabel's text appears as a group effort. The perfection of the Felsenburg civilization creates a prelapsarian paradise, but Schnabel uses the earthquake to warn that temptation *could* still pose a danger to the utopian civilization even though it never actually does.

Something a little different happens in *Simplicissimus*. Simplicius's path to salvation is not cumulative in the same way that the spiritual journeys of the protagonists in the Protestant texts are. Simplicius simply does not pass through identifiable stages of spiritual enlightenment. He makes repeated attempts to live a virtuous life, but until God picks him up and puts him on the island, these prove unsuccessful. Simplicius's experiences of the seven deadly sins and the text's hidden astrological structure seem to be the only systematic aspects of his journey. The tension in his story is not between the demands of a linear narrative and the theological dangers of reliance on works but rather between Simplicius's attempt to narrate the text as a linear and cumulative story and the impossibility of creating such a story as long as his experiences take place in a world that *is* chaotic, deceptive, and simply does not make very much sense. When the world refuses to conform to the biblical paradigm, Simplicius finds it necessary to replace this inadequate narrative with his own story. At the end of *Simplicissimus* and in *Springinsfeld* Simplicius's life story takes on the function and the characteristics of the Bible.

The Protestant texts focus on a continuous review of personal experience. Memory strengthens belief by revealing God's direct action in the life of the individual. Until he reaches the island, however, Simplicius is never able to tell his story in a complete and truthful way. He only succeeds in reviewing his *entire* life story in a very small number of cases.[11] During his trial near Wittstock, he conceals his riches. In Hanau the pastor tells his story to Governor Ramsay. Simplicius avoids telling his story to Olivier. Three conversion attempts based on his remembrance of past sins fail despite an initial promise of success. After he nearly drowns in the Rhine, Simplicius prefers to lie rather than reveal his past to his rescuers (*ST*, 320–22). In Switzerland a devil, rather than Simplicius himself, reviews Simplicius's life and past sins (*ST*, 378–79). Following Herzbruder's death, Simplicius turns from examining his past and future to examining the physical attributes of his prospective wife (*ST*, 394–95). Although he reviews his story just before the Mummelsee episode, he remains concerned about how his social role has changed and how much money he has lost during his life (*ST*, 408–9). When Simplicius finally succeeds in reviewing his life at the end of the fifth book, his ability to produce his story does not have a lasting, positive effect. Moved by remembrance and repentance, he returns to life as a hermit, but he is unable to sustain his good resolutions. By the time he reappears in the *Continuatio*, he has returned to his old, greedy ways.

A number of critics argue for an Augustinian influence on *Simplicissimus*,[12] and I have attempted to see a connection between Grimmelshausen's work and a specifically Augustinian model for the spiritual autobiography. Grimmelshausen does seem to be playing games with the expectations of his readers. Walter Busch argues that he parodies the Augustinian model during the Schermesser story,[13] and it is even possible to read Simplicius's entire narrative in the same way. It is difficult, however, to see a positive influence from Augustine on the text. As a Roman Catholic — even one with Protestant roots — Grimmelshausen displays a different understanding of original sin and redemption than the other authors, and this affects the structure of Simplicius's conversion experience and his life story.

In his book on utopias Frank Baudach describes the differences between the early modern Protestant/Augustinian and the Roman Catholic/Thomist understanding of the effects of original sin. According to Roman Catholic dogma, humans have displayed unequal intellectual and physical abilities since the time of creation. Adam's intellectual, moral, and physical attributes were gifts from God to a particular individual. God has simply not given these qualities to postlapsarian man. The flawed state of humanity is man's natural state.[14] As Baudach points out, this relatively pessimistic understanding of human nature means that Roman Catholic utopias tend to remain hierarchical. They depict a civilization that is better than the real system rather than completely ideal.[15]

The Roman Catholic position has some specific implications in the present context. Simplicius has trouble escaping material temptation, but this is the lot of mortal man. In *Simplicissimus* it is impossible for him to escape his own weakness without extraordinary supernatural assistance. He only manages to lead a virtuous life after God removes him from temptation by placing him on the island. Likewise, it is only on the island that Simplicius is able to read the Book of Nature in a mystical way. Simplicius displays his writing and reading abilities throughout his story, but it is only with divine assistance that he suddenly learns to see the connections between the empirical world and God's intentions for man in addition to the discrepancies.

Simplicius is the most passive and helpless of all of the main characters in the texts under discussion. The structure of the book reflects his repeated failure to overcome his flawed and sinful nature. His redemption cannot be cumulative because he needs supernatural intervention to escape the sinful world. Alone he can neither sustain his pious isolation nor regain Adam's prelapsarian abilities. The insights he achieves on the island do not signal a return to the natural state of man. Instead, they indicate that God has chosen to give him extra gifts. Simplicius's salvation is even more arbitrary and dependent on the hidden workings of the divine will than the salvation of any of the Protestant characters.

Simplicius's passivity has an impact on the moral function of *Simplicissimus*. An allegorical episode near the end of the *Continuatio* describes the limitations of the intended didactic function of Grimmelshausen's moral satire. A group of Dutch sailors land on Simplicius's island. They steal Simplicius's life story and they eat the fruit of a tree upon which Simplicius has inscribed a warning. Their sinful greed makes them unable to read the words on the tree properly. Eating becomes a metaphor for reading: the sailors eat the outer flesh of the fruit, and as a result they contract *Don Quixoteitis*. They understand only the part of the text that the fruit represents, without ingesting the inner kernel of truth, the moral that would complete the vision. Each sailor pictures his own fanciful desires until Simplicius returns them to their normal perceptions by giving them the inner peach kernel to eat.

This episode reflects the basic lesson Simplicius learns during his travels, namely, that folly blinds the sinful. The same lesson applies equally to readers trying to understand a text and to characters trying to understand the corrupt world. Both are books that require interpretation. In their destructive activities and their folly the sailors represent worldly man. They read the partial sense of the text, but they never understand its moral lessons. They are carried away by their imaginations but fail to apply the lessons present in the story they read to their own actions. Their odd behavior is a sign of a total absence of self-awareness, a total misunderstanding of themselves and their circumstances. Like the sugar-coated pill metaphor, the peach kernel metaphor highlights the importance of the moral lesson of the text while also showing its limitations. Reading Simplicius's story should reveal the world in its true light. The book is capable of correcting the flawed perceptions that are the product of man's sinful desires, but to progress any further in understanding creation requires God's special favor.

Throughout *Simplicissimus* Grimmelshausen uses Simplicius's lack of moral development to illustrate the limitations of human knowledge. In the first few chapters Simplicius represents man in his natural state. He is not willfully sinful, but his ignorance makes him a prisoner of the carnal world. His physical needs and appetites control him. Sitting in a tree, scared and hungry, he only responds to the pious hermit when he hears him recite a prayer that mentions food (*ST,* 21). Later, hearing the Lord's Prayer, Simplicius wishes for cheese in addition to his daily bread (*ST,* 26). Like an animal, he is a purely material being. Because of his lack of experience, he can only respond to the specific stimulus around him. Simplicius can understand concrete ideas, but he is unable to grasp abstract or transcendent concepts.

Although the hermit is one of the few kind and benevolent characters to appear in the book, he fails to teach Simplicius properly. Through his isolation and asceticism he tries to escape society and the tyranny of physical appetites, but his wholehearted rejection of the world has no positive or constructive result. Because he strives so hard to reject the material world, he remains bound to it. The hermit's spiritual concerns overpower his ability to understand his surroundings. As a result, when he encounters Simplicius he fears that devilish ghouls have come to disrupt his meditations. Because he only interprets his experiences according to his preconceived notions of what to expect and what to fear, the hermit fails to see that what he perceives is only an illusion. The lesson of this episode is the lesson the entire book, namely, "der Wahn betreügt"[16] (madness deceives). The limited perspective that results from their false desires or expectations blinds humans to their surroundings and prevents them from communicating with each other. The interactions between Simplicius and the hermit are symptomatic of what is wrong with the entire world.

In the course of his education by the hermit, Simplicius develops a literal understanding of the Bible that informs his equally literal understanding of the world. He tries to converse with pictures in the Bible. He wants to douse the fire in an illustration with real water (*ST,* 30–31). His writing mimics the appearance of the printed word (*ST,* 31). By copying out the printed text in books, Simplicius achieves only a material imitation of what should be understood spiritually. He learns to read the Bible only as a text that contains the laws that structure material existence. The hermit does not teach Simplicius that the relationship between the empirical world and the scriptural story is often problematic. Before Simplicius meets the hermit, the *wolf* is the concept that embodies all that is destructive or dangerous. Following the hermit's instruction, biblical teachings become the defining parameters for his understanding of the material world.

Initially Simplicius reads the Bible as an account of what the world is actually like rather than what it should be like. The reality he observes in Hanau simply bears no relation to biblical recommendations concerning how people should act. Simplicius sees no correspondence between what the people he meets claim to believe and how they conduct their lives (*ST,* 66). Because he reads the Bible so literally, Simplicius does not understand how easily material desires can eclipse the God-given moral code. He cannot understand why people who have read and understood the Bible do not follow its recommendations for living a moral and pious life (*ST,* 68). In his reading Simplicius has digested the text entirely. He discovers in Hanau that it is possible to read Scripture without internalizing its meaning.

A concept of language just as absolute accompanies Simplicius's literal reading. His conversations with the hermit are comical because he does not understand that a single word can have more than one meaning. A set of puns on the Ten Commandments scandalizes Simplicius in Hanau. He does not yet know how to take advantage of language's ambiguities. He also finds appalling the blasphemous oaths and curses he hears in the garrison. They disturb Simplicius because the words are so completely detached from their meanings. The men swear without thinking about what they are saying. They defile the words that Simplicius believes describe eternal truths by denying them any meaning at all.

Like the Felsenburgers and the early Quakers, Simplicius follows a literal understanding of how language should operate: yes should mean yes, and no should mean no.[17] His experiences in the world constantly reveal that language does not operate in such a straightforward fashion. In *The Pilgrim's Progress* Christian's examiners assist him to remember, organize, and learn from his past experiences. They possess a superior spiritual perspective and unfailingly ask the right questions, so Christian's understanding develops from one examination scene to the next. In Grimmelshausen's novel, however, the most constructive examination occurs during the conversation between Simplicius and the hermit in the opening pages of the text. Following this problematic beginning, Simplicius becomes aware that his own subjective perspective prevents him from being understood by each examiner, yet he is unable to discover a shared language that would permit him to reply intelligibly to those who question him. The figures of authority responsible for the interrogations are themselves victims of the disrupted communication that characterizes worldly interaction. Even when Simplicius acts virtuously, they are too sinful to understand his innocence.

During his examination by Governor Ramsay, Simplicius is sufficiently aware of his own ignorance not to give answers that his audience will not understand (*ST,* 55). Unfortunately, the governor refuses to believe that Simplicius really does not know where he has been living. Simplicius cannot describe his previous home in any way that includes a recognizable name or even a location in relation to Hanau. Simplicius is even less lucky when he is discovered in disguise near Wittstock, in part because he tries to deceive his interrogators. His audience does not allow him to tell the complete story (*ST,* 174).[18] The questions they ask him are wrong. They are the very opposite of the questions that the examiners ask Christian, in that they have no direct connection to Simplicius's own experiences and merely spring from the mistaken expectations of his examiners.

Under these constraining circumstances, Simplicius limits himself to providing intentionally incomplete answers. He provokes further inquiry by puzzling the regimental auditor. Simplicius then tells his story to the general auditor, but once again his account conflicts with the expectations of his audience. He does not mention the money hidden in the donkey's ears tied to his arms; this omission seems to show that he has lied about everything. Simplicius's auditors are so used to living in a corrupt world that they expect deception rather than honesty. It is impossible to tell the story in a way that will satisfy them. Signs of deception are intelligible in this corrupt world, whereas signs of innocence are not.

Simplicius learns to take advantage of the human propensity for mistaken interpretation in order to survive. He does this by mastering the art of deception. When Simplicius's naïveté becomes irritating to the governor, the servants of the garrison disguise themselves as devils and angels and use brainwashing techniques to transform him into a fool. During this incident Simplicius learns that is possible to think one thing yet do another. He outwardly appears to believe that his torturers really are devils while inwardly realizing that they are in disguise. For the first time there is a distance between what he sees and how he reacts to it. He describes to the reader the mental calculations that motivate his pretense (*ST,* 110).

Like the people who surround him, Simplicius distinguishes between his inner, knowing self and his outward appearance. He creates a deceptive facade to disguise his interior character. Once Simplicius recognizes the limited perspective of each individual subject, he begins to develop his ability to take advantage of man's inherent gullibility. No single truth exists in a given situation. Individuals only see what they want to see: the foolish world *wants* to be deceived (*ST,* 114). Simplicius acquires the power to manipulate his actions and language to conform to what the people around him want to believe.

Although Simplicius initially uses his powers for survival, they soon become the means of his absorption into worldly behavior. His ability to understand and mock human folly is a departure from the virtuous ignorance that characterizes his initial moral standpoint. His satirical comments on courtly dress (*ST,* 117–18) proceed from a desire to please, impress, and disturb his audience, not from a sincere wish to teach and instruct them. He does not pray in earnest, as taught by the hermit, in order to praise God but merely for appearance's sake in order to awaken the guilt and pity of his audience (*ST,* 131). Simplicius divorces his words from their meanings. He manipulates language in order to gratify his own selfish desires.

A further sign of Simplicius's moral degeneration is his sensitivity regarding his outward appearance following his transformation. He tries to get rid of his costume because he does not want to look like a fool. This vanity simply confirms his folly, for he gets into trouble precisely when he does discard the costume. The same concern with clothing leads him astray during the Jäger von Soest episode. Like so many other incidents in the novel, these tendencies reflect his subjection to the vain and carnal world. In deceiving others, he himself becomes the victim of his own deceptions. He is acting in league with rather than in opposition to sinful society[19] because he places his trust in transient appearances.

The protean nature of a world that is deceptive and asks to be deceived impresses itself on the blank slate of Simplicius's mind. He cannot resist manipulating appearances to deceive others whenever he has the opportunity. He cooks his penitential peas and fabricates complex stories for those who desire to hear them. He uses sweet words and music to indulge his lust with six bourgeois girls, only to fall victim, as a result of his acting abilities, to the lusts of the women of Paris (*ST*, 304–7). Most of his trickery as the Jäger von Soest involves physical disguise, but inventions like the listening trumpet (*ST*, 201) and his later insight into arcane arts (*ST*, 439–40) and quack medicine (*ST*, 313–16) reflect his obsession with demonstrating that things are not always as they seem. His love of deception seductively interferes with the possibility of escaping the sensory — and frequently sensual — realm.

Simplicius is more aware than most other characters that his expectations cloud his judgment. Despite his cunning, Simplicius lacks the self-awareness and ability to learn from his experiences that the hermit recommends in the first book (*ST*, 35). He develops less as a character than, say, Robinson Crusoe because he fails to learn from his mistakes in any progressive fashion. The hermit's advice and some of the episodes in the book hint that if he only reflected on the lessons his experiences teach and tried harder to lead a moral life, the world might not appear so godforsaken and chaotic.

Simplicius meets a series of priests and pastors during his journeys. Regardless of confession, they all know how to negotiate their way through the world because they understand human nature. The Reformed pastor in Lippstadt detects Simplicius's lustful preoccupations by noticing that he is reading fewer religious works and writing about sex (*ST*, 263–65). Unlike the naïve Simplicius, the pastor in Hanau knows when to shut his eyes to the sins of his flock (*ST*, 74). None of these ministers display any great degree of spiritual insight, but their calling appears to have equipped them with the practical ability to recognize the flaws in human conduct without themselves falling victim to sin.

Like the pastoral figures in *The Pilgrim's Progress*, these benevolent characters encourage Simplicius to better understand his own experiences by learning to tell his story. The pastor in Hanau makes Simplicius's story intelligible to the governor (*ST*, 58) and adds to the account of Simplicius's past by revealing the hermit's life story. The pastor in Lippstadt reads Simplicius's first literary endeavors and encourages him to pursue his work as an author.

The chaplain in Philippsburg asks him for his confession (*ST*, 325). The superior knowledge that these pastoral figures display indicates that it may be possible for some pious individuals to reconcile their personal conduct in the carnal world with a Christian moral position.

The sense that Simplicius's experiences are part of a greater or longer story appears throughout *Simplicissimus*. When some of the old Herzbruder's predictions come true, it appears as though some sort of destiny is at work in Simplicius's life even if he is unwilling to admit it (*ST*, 167). Grimmelshausen uses prophetic incidents to demonstrate how Simplicius's excessive confidence in his own abilities blinds him to his true identity. Although in *Simplicissimus* all predictions concerning future occurrences come true, this foreknowledge is of limited use. The hermit's letter (*ST*, 51) preserves Simplicius and the pastor in the short term, but it becomes impossible for Simplicius to follow the hermit's last recommendations in such a predatory world. Hanau is anything but comfortable. It is in the garrison there that Simplicius understands the pastor's warning against future danger and pride, although, being on the lookout for hypocrisy, he falsely ascribes the warning to the pastor's self-interest. Later he heeds the predictions of the Wahrsagerin of Soest in order to safeguard his wealth, perhaps because the warnings accord with his desire to secure his treasure. This is only of limited use since he disregards her further warnings regarding the dangers of lust. At first this is the result of his ignorance; he is still young and does not yet recognize the power of carnal desire. Lacking self-awareness, despite the warnings he slips into sin without noticing what he is doing. Prognostication, however successful, reveals only a portion of the entire truth. Simplicius's limited perspective obscures his ability to interpret the future correctly.

The problem of Simplicius's identity appears in connection with the prophecy motif. He is explicitly told about his noble birth three times. The old Herzbruder and the Wahrsagerin of Soest include partial revelations of Simplicius's identity in their prophecies. Simplicius does not believe them because he thinks his Knan is his real father (*ST*, 167). Later he rejects the possibility that he is of noble birth at the very moment when he is most preoccupied with pretending that he *is* noble and longing for livery for his servants (*ST*, 237, 244–45). Simplicius discovers a hoard of enchanted treasure that seems to fulfill an ancient saying (*ST*, 242), but even this fails to resolve the identity problem. He focuses on hiding the treasure and does not stop to consider whether the prophecy might apply to him. His identity stays hidden and the story remains incomplete. When Simplicius finally does discover the truth about his birth, it is too late and the knowledge is of no use. Contrary to the expectations set up during the fairy-tale-like hidden treasure episode, his noble birth never has a positive effect on his story. In *Simplicissimus* the world is so deceptive that it is impossible to achieve the single, simple dissolution of false appearances that reveals hidden identities in fairy tales or in popular romances. Simplicius's sinfulness makes him ignorant of his noble birth, just as it makes him unaware of his relationship with God, his heavenly father.

Simplicius's story fails to follow the conventions of established genres, even though it continually hints that events in Simplicius's life are meant to fulfill some greater destiny. The work defies the expectations set up by its use of some of the conventions of popular romance, just as Simplicius's frequent attempts to escape the world and live a more pious life invoke the teleological structure and the forward impetus of spiritual autobiography. The failure of different models to structure Simplicius's experiences is a sign of the corruption of creation. Events in a world that is so chaotic simply do not conform to the definite beginning, middle, and end that characterizes events in structured literary genres.

Is there any sense of progress in Simplicius's story? There is no real progression in terms of spiritual enlightenment. Until the very end of the *Continuatio,* Simplicius simply does not draw nearer to God as a result of his experiences. If anything, he seems to move farther away. The increasingly frantic motion of his journeys toward the end of the first volume and in the *Continuatio* reflect this spiritual distance. Simplicius does experience a religious conversion and reforms his wicked ways, but this happens very suddenly, and it does not occur as a result of any systematic, linear, spiritual, or psychological development.

The way an audience misreads a text can sometimes be just as informative as more correct interpretations. It is easy to see how some critics find it possible to read the book, or portions of it, in connection with Augustinian thought even though the whole point of the story is that Simplicius does not progress gradually toward salvation but requires an extraordinary divine intervention in order to reform his wicked ways. The text partially echoes the structure of Augustinian spiritual autobiography (for example, the split between the pious narrator and the ignorant, experiencing self), only to disappoint readers' expectations by depicting religious conversion as a sudden event rather than a linear, cumulative process. Readers keep expecting Simplicius to reform because they know from his commentary that he eventually becomes more moral, but fortune, not God, rules his life before he reaches the island.

It is also quite possible to misread the text from a more secular viewpoint. Recent Grimmelshausen criticism has not been particularly kind to those early critics who managed to misread *Simplicissimus* sufficiently to label it a Bildungsroman,[20] but the storytelling episodes in the text reveal the source of their misunderstanding. The book includes a loose and rather uneven sense of development in terms of Simplicius's abilities to use language and tell stories. In an overenthusiastic attempt to define a completely German contribution to the history of the novel, early critics confused this sense of development with the depiction of the progressive calling of the artist in the Bildungsroman. It is, of course, nothing of the sort. Simplicius learns how to tell better stories as he grows older, but his ability is useless — even destructive — without the spiritual enlightenment that would give his narrative its rightful purpose. Very much a man of his own time, Grimmelshausen is in no way a closet Romantic — but he does depict narration as a force with the power to damn or to save. Eventually — particularly in *Springinsfeld* — storytelling almost becomes a new religion.

Throughout most of the novel Grimmelshausen uses episodes that include storytelling to demonstrate the deficiencies in Simplicius's moral and spiritual state. The way Simplicius describes his experiences at the beginning of the novel reveals his complete ignorance. His description of the pillaging of the farm in the first book is grotesque yet very powerful because he does not understand that the soldiers are behaving cruelly. Later his ability to speak satirically when he makes fun of court dress demonstrates that he has learned to recognize vice. Simplicius's writing reflects his fascination with sin. His account of Joseph's temptations foreshadows his own sexual misadventures (*ST*, 265). His ability to dream up and organize stories other than his autobiography (which he always has difficulty telling) seems to vary inversely with his moral degeneration.

Although Grimmelshausen often depicts the ability to manipulate language as a devilish or demonic attribute (as in the story of Olivier, Simplicius's alter ego), reading and storytelling are also central to Simplicius's conversion. The ability to tell stories has a positive as well as a negative potential. Simplicius's storytelling activities become more frequent near the end of the first volume and in the *Continuatio*. These episodes reflect his ability to organize a narrative, understand the world around him, and interpret the words and signs he encounters during his journey. Yet they also reveal Simplicius's ability to use his imagination for the wrong reasons. By contrasting the stories he tells prior to his conversion with the narrative skills he displays afterward, Grimmelshausen reveals how the island alters Simplicius's ability to understand stories and his skill in generating them.

The Mummelsee episode teaches an important lesson: irony and deception, the disjunction between words and their meanings, dishonest discourse, and incomplete stories are the products of the Fall. The sylphs use language in an unambiguous way because they are perfectly reasonable and immune to sin. The king of the sylphs cannot understand Simplicius's description of a nonexistent, perfect world as a satire of the real one. The sylphs only use a single system of meanings. They possess a comprehensive knowledge of the material realm, but they are unable to understand spiritual things because they have no souls (*ST,* 417). In contrast, Simplicius displays demonic characteristics when he manipulates language by using lies, puns, secret codes, satire, and irony.

Although Simplicius's misuse of language shows his fallen nature, his power over words also indicates his positive spiritual potential. The king of the sylphs appeals to Simplicius for news of God's plans for creation. He expects Simplicius to possess a level of insight into the workings of the divine mind that he, as a being without a soul, is incapable of attaining (*ST,* 425). By using his imagination, Simplicius can generate stories that move beyond material, empirical evidence; moreover, he can understand his experiences from different perspectives. According to the sylph king, Simplicius should be capable of reaching an enlightened perspective that would give him some insight into how his spiritual destiny relates to God's plans for creation.

Simplicius's sylph guide answers his questions with a precise description of the history of the sylphs and their position on the continuum of creation. The sylphs also tell Simplicius what they know about human nature and human destiny (*ST,* 433). Simplicius understands what the sylphs say, just as he understands the contrast between the world that he describes and the world as it should be. He does not learn from either of these stories, however, because he fails to apply their lessons to his own experience. His desire for profit makes him ignorant,[21] preventing him from drawing a moral either from the stories he tells or those he hears.

At the beginning of the *Continuatio,* Simplicius's speculations concerning the nature of sin result in a dream, the odd story of Julus and Avarus. Like most of the examples of storytelling in the *Continuatio,* the value of this episode is ambiguous. On the one hand, Simplicius's dream has a fairly organized structure. The story is obviously an allegory, seeming to come from some source outside of Simplicius himself. Speaking as the retrospective narrator, Simplicius makes it clear that it is meant to teach a moral lesson (*ST,* 489). On the other hand, Simplicius dreams about the story not out of any concern with moral improvement but because he starts thinking about sin when he is bored. Although he comments on the meaning of the story from the point of view of the retrospective narrator, at the time he has the vision Simplicius hardly pays attention to its meaning and fails to apply the moral lesson to the story of his own life. Grimmelshausen uses this allegorical tale to bolster his argument concerning the didactic value of the text, but as a reader of his vision Simplicius shows that he remains trapped by material concerns.

The next episode concerned with narrative is Simplicius's meeting with Baldanders. The Baldanders episode states the theme of the novel as a whole: change is the only thing that is unchanging in the postlapsarian world (*ST,* 467). Simplicius's reference to Hans Sachs (*ST,* 506) shows that Baldanders is a fictional character. He is not intended to be a realistic figure. Instead, Grimmelshausen makes him the vehicle for a very direct, didactic lesson concerning the meaning of the text. Baldanders is an emblematic figure, an allegory for Simplicius and the reader to interpret. He transforms his appearance many times, telling Simplicius that he represents the change that is the defining constant in all of Simplicius's diverse experiences. Baldanders describes how the events in Simplicius's life reflect the general principle that nothing is certain or unchanging. While this is a pessimistic lesson, Simplicius's ability to see how this general lesson or moral relates to his personal experience shows an improvement in his self-awareness in comparison to earlier episodes in the novel.

Simplicius's suspicions during the Baldanders episode reflect the association between the misuse of language and the devil that appears throughout Grimmelshausen's text. Simplicius initially interprets the nonsensical words in the message as an evil spell (*ST,* 508). In fact, Baldanders and his message are morally ambiguous, even benevolent. When Simplicius deciphers the message, it tells him to converse with inanimate objects by using his imagination. Like Robinson Crusoe, Simplicius's curiosity about his surroundings tends to get him into trouble. Baldanders's lesson is that in order to satisfy his curiosity he must learn to make up stories. The key to understanding the world lies in imagination, not mere observation.

Simplicius's actions following the Baldanders episode reflect the ambiguous nature of his mastery of language. He enjoys cracking the code in which the message is written, but he does not pause to consider its meaning. His interpretation of the life of Saint Alexius shows how he misreads the signs that appear in order to instruct him. Simplicius begins to read hagiographic texts as much to pass the time as for their exemplary value. He interprets the Saint Alexius story as a message to urge him to return to a life of wandering in the world, but he emulates Saint Alexius in a material rather than a spiritual way. He imagines what his life as a hermit might be like in winter and decides that it will be much easier to go on a pilgrimage. Simplicius fails to take advantage of the insights that the vision of Baldanders provides. He certainly does not consciously understand that the role of the imagination is to read the stories hidden in the world and to extrapolate general moral lessons from them.

Storytelling fills Simplicius's pilgrimage, but he tells stories for the wrong reasons. He is a practiced liar, fabricating his stories in order to please his listeners. He does not tell his stories to teach but rather to entertain and bribe his listeners into helping him. On the positive side, Simplicius does show that he can use his imagination and effectively organize raw material based on his own experiences or from books by other authors. Nonetheless, in his entertaining fictions Simplicius demonstrates that he has not yet reached the level of narrative competence he demonstrates as the retrospective narrator of *Simplicissimus*. The stories he tells are not empirically, allegorically, or morally true. At this stage his stories neither inform nor improve his audience; they merely deceive them.

Simplicius practices Baldanders's art in the Schermesser episode, but he fails to realize its full potential. He draws no moral from the conversation. The story remains a mere chain of cause-and-effect transformations. It lacks the teleological and explicit moral interpretations that would organize it and give it meaning. The Schermesser eventually becomes a journal of accounts, a register of material goods rather than a narrative. The steward treats the book as his bible. He writes in it to cover up his misdeeds (*ST*, 521). Like Olivier and the secretary in Hanau, the steward uses his literacy to hide his trickery rather than to recognize and repudiate it. His account records what he has not done. This is just the opposite of a spiritual autobiography, which records and interprets events that have happened. The author of the account book fails to overcome his material desires or to understand the greater lessons taught by his individual experiences. His book ends up in the dunghill where it belongs.

In telling the Schermesser story, Simplicius fails to relate each individual event to a greater whole. The story reaches no point of rest and no concluding perspective that could provide it with meaning. The nominal ending of the story is in the toilet, but Simplicius's lack of mercy really dooms the Schermesser to continuing change. When he becomes a lump of used toilet paper, the Schermesser returns to the cycle of decay and transformation that has characterized his entire story. In carrying out his judgment, Simplicius fails to see the parallel between his life of constant material change and the Schermesser's pathetic existence. He does not apply the general principle of the story — namely, that a life of endless material change simply ends on the dunghill — to his own narrative. He does not listen to the Schermesser's final warning (*ST*, 521–22), dooming him without considering that he might also be dooming himself.

Simplicius's failure to heed the warning of a story that he himself has generated only emphasizes his imprisonment in the earthly, dung-filled world. He has the power to tell stories and he can make inanimate objects speak, but he cannot apply even the negative principles that lie behind worldly experience to his own existence. His attachment to the world prevents him from seeing the lesson his life teaches: material existence is meaningless and change is a constant state in the postlapsarian world. Simplicius does not understand these negative lessons well enough to begin to worry about whether any positive alternative exists.

Although Simplicius does not pass through the same psychological stages of conversion as the main characters in the other novels, being shipwrecked on the island does lead to his sudden conversion. As a result of the insight that accompanies his miraculous preservation, he no longer moves through a world that makes no sense. His survival shows him that God has singled him out for special care and assistance. On the island, if nowhere else, Simplicius can see evidence of God's intervention in his life. His survival seems to be part of a greater divine plan. Time becomes meaningful. Simplicius demonstrates that he has escaped the constant flux that characterized his life in the world when he begins carefully keeping track of the days. He even sets aside Sundays for godly conversation (*ST*, 562). Simplicius's new definition of himself as a chosen individual makes it easier for him to maintain his faith and his good intentions. It makes it possible for him to tell his life story as one having a specific ending, namely, his spiritual redemption and physical salvation on a paradisiacal island.

After Simon Meron's death, living on the island means that Simplicius lives completely removed from the selfish corruption of his fellow humans. He can sustain his virtuous way of life because he is not part of human society. His isolation allows him to escape his former frantic movement up and down the social ladder. The island's limited size makes it impossible for him to travel too far. The devilish Abyssinian woman and Simon Meron's early death warn Simplicius that he could still fall prey to temptation. He also says that his variable thoughts cause him difficulties, but change and temptation are weaker forces thanks to his isolation and pose less of a danger. His physical stability on the island provides him with a secure mental and moral perspective from which to read and understand the value of his past experiences.

Simplicius also develops an ability to read the Book of Nature as a result of his isolation on the island. If he is a chosen individual, then God speaks to him through his experiences. If God has spoken to him by putting him on the island, then his experiences and even his physical surroundings reveal further information about God's plans. Since he has no books, Simplicius learns to read his surroundings instead.

Simplicius's reading of nature is not subject to the linear, materialistic infinity that characterizes the Schermesser's narrative. Simplicius puts religious inscriptions on trees in assorted languages and symbolic characters to remind himself that the finite world reveals truths that are spiritual and transcendent (*ST*, 573). He recognizes that an infinity of meanings is present within each created object since all of creation reflects an infinite God. Simplicius uses the whole of his linguistic knowledge, but his inscriptions still only hint at the great glory of the highest Good (*ST*, 573).

Simplicius's ability to bring out the spiritual meaning latent in empirical objects confirms that he has regained the Adamic language. The island is his book and the trees are its pages. Simplicius treats the objects around him as emblems; read together, they form a magical, symbolic, natural *Ursprache*. He has mastered allegoresis in the sense that he has learned to see the comprehensive spiritual meaning that lies behind individual objects and individual words. From the Jäger of Soest episodes onward, Simplicius displays an encyclopedic level of knowledge, but his hitherto undisclosed ability to write in six languages — including ancient and biblical languages — further indicates that he has developed a communicative talent that reverses the effects of Babel.

There is another important aspect to Simplicius's ability to read his world. Near the beginning of the novel, the hermit's nightingale song describes how all of creation praises God. Each creature sings in its own way, using its God-given voice. Because man is made in the image of God, Simplicius recognizes himself as an author or creator, a second God, when he recognizes God as the creator. By producing stories that re-create the empirical world, he mirrors God's creative and generative activity. Like his mystical reading of the Book of Nature, this is a form of praise. He writes his autobiography to record his experiences as well as to point up for the benefit of his readers the disparity between how the world should work and how it does work. He also writes his autobiography because writing is magic. It is creative and thus has a great transforming power.

By writing his autobiography, Simplicius becomes godlike. As the retrospective narrator of his life story, he creates a world in which experiences do make sense. They lead, however indirectly, toward a specific goal and take place against a framework of specific moral and spiritual values. He learns to control and learn from his experiences because his knowledge is no longer limited. He gains authority in relation to his readers when he explains the moral lessons derived from his experiences. By writing his own life story, he sets in motion a web of storytelling activity that takes on a life of its own. Characters from his own story read and react to his narrative. He does not merely re-create his own world by telling his experiences but creates an entire, autonomous reality.

Simplicius reaches a state of spiritual enlightenment on the island, but this is not a state of mind that his readers can imitate without divine assistance. The fictional first readers of his story, Jean Cornelissen and the Dutch chaplain, do not share his insights even though they read his story sympathetically. The captain's appreciative reading contrasts with the misreading of his crew. Like other exemplary readers (for example, the dreamer, Crusoe's English captain, or Eberhard Julius), Cornelissen follows a path from limited knowledge to a greater but still imperfect understanding as a result of his reading. His description of the encounter with Simplicius shows the positive effect of reading Simplicius's story. He describes his lack of comprehension when he originally read the messages on the trees (*ST,* 573), but by the time he tells the story, he displays a fair understanding of their meaning. Because he reads Simplicius's story before telling his own, the captain learns to understand the messages and the riddle of Simplicius's identity.

Although he reads sympathetically, Cornelissen's insight remains somewhere between true enlightenment and supreme ignorance. Initially he becomes lost in the cave, which, according to Hubert Gersch, is an allegorical representation of the search for divine light.[22] Cornelissen represents the reader of the work, a person informed enough to recognize the moral significance of the text but so trapped in worldly life as to require instruction and desire self-improvement. Cornelissen's account of his experiences appears reliable because of his conventional morality, his straightforward worldview, and his limited understanding. Although he provides a positive description of Simplicius — eyewitness proof of Simplicius's spiritual enlightenment — he understands Simplicius as a wonder or a novelty rather than as a purveyor of moral lessons. He prizes Simplicius's life story as a curiosity more worthy of attention than any of the objects he has collected on his journey. Cornelissen does not seem to take the moral aspect of the text very seriously, but his story does show that he is learning to interpret his experiences by following Simplicius's model. Reading has the positive effect of turning him into a narrator himself. He writes his own story in order to tell his readers why Simplicius's book is so valuable and so interesting.

Although Simplicius's story in the *Continuatio* ends on a positive and pious note, Jean Cornelissen's narrative reveals that there are still problems in Simplicius's paradisiacal way of life. Contact with his fellow man remains dangerous. Unlike Crusoe or the Felsenburgers, he has not created a positive, alternative society on the island. Simplicius's way of life is positive *only* because God has helped him to escape the many evils of the sinful world (*ST*, 584). *Simplicissimus* and the *Continuatio* never resolve this sense of isolation. *Simplicissimus* also displays a marked difficulty with closure. Readers of the book know that Simplicius's attempts to maintain a pious withdrawal from the world have already failed several times, and this makes it difficult to place any faith in the permanence of his state of illumination and rest on the island.

Simplicius engages the reader's sympathy, but unlike most of the protagonists in the other works, he is not a representative character. While he is in a state of sin, he is more capable of cunning and deception than most characters in the novel. He has more authority once God removes him from temptation and restores the intellectual powers and physical attributes that originally belonged to Adam. Throughout the final episode Grimmelshausen depicts Simplicius as a Christ figure thanks to his great knowledge and mysterious abilities. By curing the sick sailors, he mimics Christ's healing in the

Bible. In the same episode he appears to the captain as a light shining in the darkness. The Dutch chaplain mediates between Simplicius and the sailors just as, more conventionally, he would play a mediating role between God and his congregation. He tells the other officers that Simplicius has reached the highest level of spiritual understanding possible to man (*ST,* 573) and declares that Simplicius lives directly under God's protection. The sailors have risked God's wrath by attempting to harm him. Even more extraordinary is the fact that the chaplain preaches a sermon in which he praises all of God's miracles but singles Simplicius out for praise above them all (*ST,* 582). Simplicius assumes a messianic role because of his healing and creative powers.

The Dutch captain and chaplain can see that Simplicius has reached a state of spiritual enlightenment, but they are unable to reach a similar level themselves. While reading Simplicius's narrative might help them identify what is wrong with the world, it does not aid them in understanding how the world reveals the workings of God. Seeing Simplicius from their perspective is like reading the ending of Robinson Crusoe's story from the perspective of the English captain and the mutineers: Simplicius appears superhuman and his power over his surroundings seems miraculous because neither these characters nor the book's readers understand how he knows what he does.

Unlike *The Pilgrim's Progress, Simplicissimus* is not a guide to salvation. Simplicius's path is impossible to follow or imitate. It is too wide-ranging, too strange, too dependent on Simplicius himself. Simplicius's linguistic competence and his mastery of numerous arts show that he is more powerful — and therefore more authoritative — than the reader. His strange appearance, noble background, and wit and cunning also set him apart. The doubts cast on Simplicius's honesty as a result of his ability to manipulate language and his frequent references to his false stories create additional distance between the narrator and the reader. Instead of revealing his development as a character, Simplicius's experiences simply reflect the many ghastly variations on human sinfulness.

Despite the description of his spiritual and moral reformation, paradoxes also appear in Simplicius's attitude toward religion at the end of *Simplicissimus.* In the early stages of his island sojourn his only wish connected with institutional Christianity is for spiritual books and a Bible. These become unnecessary once he replaces them with his own reading of his surroundings and writing of his experiences. Although ostensibly Roman

Catholic, Simplicius rejects the institutional church and its sacraments. He says he will have no need for the prayers of a fellow Christian in his dying hour. When given the opportunity to ask the Dutch crew for a Bible, he does not do so. Instead he requests glasses for the purely material reason that he can use them to make a fire. Instead of receiving books, he gives the sailors his own narrative. Jean Cornelissen says that the sailors and officers of the ship worship Simplicius like an idol for his healing abilities (*ST*, 583). Grimmelshausen acknowledges that Simplicius is usurping the role of the divine author.

When Simplicius appears again in *Der seltzame Springinsfeld*, he retains the enlightenment and overarching perspective he achieved on the island. Springinsfeld's rude comments[23] indicate that Simplicius has changed dramatically since they last met. He now resembles a saint and talks like a preacher. He demonstrates near-magical abilities when he purifies wine while Springinsfeld and Philarchus look on. The transformation has obvious religious connotations. In addition to the sacramental reference, Simplicius's ability to make good wine from bad shows that he is able to purge his surroundings of corruption. At the beginning of *Simplicissimus* the hermit warns Simplicius about the dangers of bad company. Good wine poured into vinegar goes bad (*ST*, 35). When he transforms the wine, Simplicius reverses this process and shows that he has the power to redeem the bad people around him.[24] The purified wine is the color of gold — a sign of perfection — and the wine itself is a sign that Simplicius is a savior, able to return the world around him to its prelapsarian state.

If Christ's story as related in the Bible has the power to reconcile man and God, Simplicius's story has the power to correct the relationship between man and the world. The skills Simplicius brings with him from the island are related to his abilities to cure the Dutch sailors' delusions. By exerting his storytelling abilities, he reveals the way sin makes his fellow humans misread their surroundings. The emblems in the *Gaukeltasche* reflect the desires of whoever looks into the book, but Simplicius insists that his art is natural, not magical. In the first book of *Simplicissimus* the hermit tells Simplicius that he should grow in self-knowledge by learning to interpret his experiences. The *Gaukeltasche* fulfills the same function as Simplicius's story: it is a *Narrenspiegel* in which his audience should learn to recognize themselves. The pictures reflect the particular weaknesses of individual onlookers. Simplicius's satirical commentary purges these readers of folly and helps them to achieve self-awareness.

Simplicius uses the *Gaukeltasche* to lead Springinsfeld toward salvation. In order to learn how to use the book to teach others, Springinsfeld must first use the pictures contained therein to understand the moral and spiritual significance of his own story. At the beginning of the work Springinsfeld is a man of action. Rather than imitating God by learning to read his experiences and retelling them in a rational and meaningful way, Springinsfeld produces a meaningless string of animal noises. Like Simplicius's life story, the book of emblems provides the material for a series of moral lessons. Learning how to interpret them is the first stage in a process leading to repentance and religious conversion (*SP*, 48). It is only when he reaches this basic state of interpretive competence that Springinsfeld becomes capable of ordered, rational communication.

Grimmelshausen limits salvation in *Simplicissimus* to the title character himself, but he depicts Simplicius as the spiritual savior of others in *Springinsfeld*. Simplicius's disastrous interactions with humanity in *Simplicissimus* constantly frustrate his attempts to lead a virtuous life. Simplicius can only generate a true, comprehensive narrative once he has been physically removed from society, when no fellow humans appear to disrupt his perspective and his interpretation, and when he understands how God looks after him. Despite this mistrust of humanity, the narrative produced on the island, Simplicius's life story, eventually creates a narrative community similar to those in the *Wunderliche Fata* and *The Pilgrim's Progress*. In *Der seltzame Springinsfeld*, if not in *Simplicissimus* itself, storytelling acts as a socially constructive force. By telling his life story, Simplicius begins to overcome his former isolation and prepares the world for his return.

Springinsfeld shows how Simplicius's story heals the disruption and lack of sympathy that formerly characterized human communication by creating a positive connection between Simplicius and his audience. In depicting this process, Grimmelshausen moves beyond the criticism of society based on Christian moral norms that appeared in *Simplicissimus*. He creates a positive alternative to worldly life, but he does so by replacing the process of reading the Bible and following its teachings — a totally hopeless endeavor, according to Simplicius's life story — with reading and imitating Simplicius's book. Through his exemplary readers and narrators, Philarchus and Springinsfeld, Simplicius offers his readers a path to salvation and moral reform that affirms the value of worldly experience.

In *Springinsfeld* Simplicius founds a community based on honest communication and sympathetic listening, whereas little or no prospect of social integration appears in *Simplicissimus*. Simplicius's interaction with his real father, the hermit, is sympathetic, but the latter teaches Simplicius only a portion of his knowledge. He hides his identity and his knowledge of the wicked world from Simplicius. He refuses to contact his friend and brother-in-law in Hanau (*ST,* 65), and he abandons Simplicius to the world when he dies. Simplicius lies several times during his friendship with Herzbruder. His good intentions frequently interfere with the straightforward communication necessary for a trusting relationship. Even on the island, Simon Meron first plots Simplicius's murder (*ST,* 557–59) and then succumbs to the lures of palm wine (*ST,* 565) rather than working with Simplicius to achieve anything like the perfect social integration present on the Insel Felsenburg. Perhaps the single most unambiguously positive, if rather comical, relationship in *Simplicissimus* is that between Simplicius and his Knan. Although simple, Simplicius's foster father is a competent farmer and Simplicius entrusts him with the management of his property.

In *Springinsfeld* Simplicius's foster family forms the core of the pleasant society that surrounds Simplicius. The members of the household welcome Springinsfeld and Philarchus into their circle because they are fellow storytellers and friends of Simplicius. Philarchus's description of the household shows that its members have overcome the misunderstanding and disrupted communication that used to be part of almost all social interaction. This social integration is not based on ties of blood — Simplicius's Knan and Meuder are not his real parents — but on mutual love, respect, and trust. The sense of community comes as a relief after the relentless pessimism of *Simplicissimus*. Perhaps most positively of all, the small community is firmly anchored at the family farm. Springinsfeld suffers the same chronic displacement as Courage and Simplicius, but the small community provides him with a final resting place. The conclusion of the story confirms that Springinsfeld and Simplicius have reached a state of rest that is at once social, physical, and spiritual. Telling true and complete stories to a sympathetic audience creates harmonious relationships.

Simplicius's concern with plain language reflects the values of his small community. In *Springinsfeld* he consciously returns to the attitude he maintained toward language during the Hanau episode in *Simplicissimus*. Several times he rebukes Springinsfeld's frivolous swearing (*SP,* 16). Utilitarian principles accompany his rejection of empty signifiers. When his money-making skills amaze Springinsfeld, Simplicius emphasizes that he is not a sorcerer who conjures the material for his tricks out of thin air. Hard work and preparation have gone into concocting the wine-purifying solution. Such a direct relationship between hard work and good money never appears in Simplicius's life story. In *Simplicissimus* the people who work the hardest, the farmers, have the worst luck, whereas the laziest and trickiest people are usually the most successful. Simplicius also condemns gratuitously ornamented language. When Philarchus couches his question in roundabout, polite speech, Simplicius criticizes his method of questioning and answers with an anecdote condemning frenchified expressions (*SP,* 20–21). As in the *Wunderliche Fata,* in *Springinsfeld* plain speech consists of a direct narrative grounded in *deutsche Redlichkeit.* There must always be a direct connection between a word or a sign and its meaning. Moreover, hard work and good intentions lead directly to material and spiritual rewards.

Simplicius does not just save his fellow humans by criticizing their moral flaws. His own story has tremendous creative and redemptive power. He uses storytelling as a kind of yeast to uplift the society around him. Through storytelling ignorance becomes knowledge. By means of storytelling Simplicius builds up a network of interrelated stories that create a world — real to the stories' characters, fictional to their readers — in which personal experiences really do reflect Christian moral principles. Courage's story is the first sequel to *Simplicissimus* after the *Continuatio.* It is written explicitly as a parody of Simplicius's narrative of redemption. Courage finishes her account completely unreformed and unrepentant, but in the process of narrating her story she shows that she is a sinner who has consciously chosen sin. She commits evil even though she knows how to do good. When she describes herself as wicked and destined for damnation, she is interpreting her experiences according to the same set of moral values and judgments as the characters in *Springinsfeld,* even though her story fails to reach a similar conclusion.

In *Springinsfeld* the conversation that leads to Springinsfeld's life story begins because of the previous stories of Simplicius and Courage. As the writer of Courage's story, Philarchus is responsible for a work unfavorable to both Simplicius and Springinsfeld. They greet him with suspicion, which he overcomes by reciting his own story truthfully. He proves that Courage has taken advantage of him too (*SP,* 38). The differences between Simplicius's and Courage's story appear in his description. Courage's story is not structured in the same way. It does not end in salvation. It has no positive moral effect on the reader. Indeed, Courage's pernicious influence has interfered with Philarchus's ability to understand Simplicius's story correctly (*SP,* 22).

After reading Simplicius's book, Philarchus has only learned one practical lesson, namely, yield to those more powerful than yourself. He learns the lesson on the spot from his own experience because Courage *is* more powerful. Reading Simplicius's story only confirms the lesson. He observes how Simplicius escapes from dangerous situations during the individual episodes of the text, but he does not absorb the moral criticism that Simplicius includes in his retrospective commentary.

By following Courage's orders, Philarchus writes a book whose content contradicts its structure. He has succeeded in imitating the form of the earlier autobiography, but he has not learned the same lessons that Simplicius learned by writing his narrative. Philarchus's inability to read Simplicius's story properly appears when he asks to hear more pranks from Simplicius's past. He is impressed by the transformation of Simplicius from a raw and godless scamp to a reputable householder (*SP*, 52). His reading has focused on the less savory elements of the tale rather than on its conclusion or moral.

Despite Philarchus's misreading of Simplicius's story, their shared profession almost immediately establishes an association between the two narrators. As the beginning of the novel illustrates, Philarchus, like Simplicius, plays a passive and dependent role in society. Although he shares the same profession he has not yet reached the equivalent stage of moral enlightenment. Philarchus is important because he occupies the middle ground between the reader and Simplicius. He is an exemplary reader of the stories of Simplicius, Courage, and Springinsfeld, but he is also a writer. He may share Simplicius's ability to use language and may demonstrate a similar potential for insight, but when he first appears he displays only rudimentary skills in interpreting what he reads and writes. By observing how Springinsfeld comes to tell his story and the effects this story has on him, he reveals how it is possible to move from a limited, flawed understanding of the world to a more enlightened state. Philarchus learns how to read the world in a positive way by following Simplicius's advice and by observing and recording Springinsfeld's good example. He also learns an important professional lesson: the whole world — or, rather, this whole fictional world — is composed of a web of stories. Each individual has a story to tell, and the secret to escaping from the cold, cruel outside world is to listen to them. Reading and telling stories creates warmth and harmonious social relationships.

When Springinsfeld participates in the exchange of stories at the inn, telling his own life story makes him aware of his weaknesses and failings. Like Simplicius and Courage, his experiences in the world reflect an endless, restless motion. His story does not have any positive spiritual destination. It lacks meaning because it lacks direction. Springinsfeld appears outwardly satisfied with simply fulfilling his material needs, yet after telling his story he appeals to Simplicius for advice about how to live another, better kind of life (*SP*, 131). Simplicius finishes Springinsfeld's story by providing him with a final goal. He urges him to start thinking about his eternal salvation and invites him to join his pleasant community for the winter in the hope of effecting a lasting conversion.

Simplicius provides a physical and social resting place for Springinsfeld, and commissions Philarchus to write the story. By means of writing, Philarchus, like Springinsfeld, learns how the final ending of the tale — Springinsfeld's conversion — gives his entire story meaning and structure. He rounds off his account in a very satisfactory way when he uses Springinsfeld's mortal end, his pious death, to end the novel:

> Wie ich mir aber seithero sagen lassen / so hat ihn der verwichne Mertz auffgeriben / nach dem er zuvor durch Simplicissimum in seinen alten Tagen gantz anders umbgegossen und ein Christlichs und bessers Leben zuführen bewögt worden; nahm also diser abenteurliche Springinsfeld auff des eben so seltzamen Simplicissimi Bauerhoff (als er ihn zuvor zu seinem Erben eingesetzt) sein letztes ENDE. (*SP*, 132)

> [As I have since heard, the past March killed him, but not until after he was moved by Simplicissimus to lead a more Christian and a better life in his old age; so this adventurous Springinsfeld met his end at the farm of the equally odd Simplicissimus (whom he had earlier appointed his heir.)]

Philarchus swaps the adjectives that describe Simplicius and Springinsfeld in the titles of their respective novels. The exchange confirms both the shared moral conclusion and the shared structure of Simplicius and Springinsfeld's life stories. They have reached a common ending, namely, spiritual conversion and membership in a positive social community. These specific stories are variations of a more universal narrative structure, according to which all life stories end in salvation or damnation.

While Springinsfeld's death gives his story closure, there is also a pleasant sense of continuity and inclusion in this ending. Like the real readers of the novel, Philarchus is a passive observer of the interactions between Springinsfeld and Simplicius. However, by hearing the story he gains admission to Simplicius's community. His interaction with Simplicius extends beyond the end of Springinsfeld's narrative. He later hears about Springinsfeld's reformation and death and is able to give his story a proper conclusion. Springinsfeld's story is over, but Simplicius's story extends into the future in an indefinite, happy state. This is like the ending to part 2 of *The Pilgrim's Progress*. The harmonious community appears to exclude conflict, leaving readers with no sense that there are more interesting episodes of the story still to come. At the same time, because this community is founded on the positive relationship between storytellers and their audience, the community appears to include both Philarchus and the real reader beyond the ending of this individual story.

The structure of Simplicius's life story at first appears as an arbitrary collection of episodes set in a world completely lacking in unity. Through its sequels, the *Simplicianische Schriften* (Simplician Novels), Simplicius's narrative becomes the center — both as a narrative model and in terms of content — for the organized and interconnected pattern of narratives that revolve around it. The narrators and scribes who react to Simplicius's account (Courage, Springinsfeld, Philarchus, and the two protagonists in *Das wunderbarliche Vogel-Nest* [The Enchanted Bird's-Nest, 1672, 1675]) create a community of stories that makes the fictional world they describe more convincing. The discussion group in the *Rathstübel Plutonis* (The Art of Getting Rich, 1672) represents the relationship between *Simplicissimus* and the other *Simplicianische Schriften*. *Simplicissimus* remains at the heart of a community of individual stories. The works share common themes and characters, and have a similar structure, but the specific details of the stories — and the value of the advice the works provide — vary according to the personalities of the individuals who tell them.

Notes

[1] The inscription "Der Wahn betreügt" (madness deceives) appears in the illustrations to some seventeenth-century editions of *Simplicissimus*. See Jan Hendrik Scholte, *Der Simplicissimus und sein Dichter: Gesammelte Aufsätze* (Tübingen: Niemeyer, 1950), 247–48.

[2] "daß Unbeständigkeit / Allein beständig sey" (that the only constant thing is inconstancy). Hans Jakob Christoph von Grimmelshausen, *Der Abentheurliche Simplicissimus Teutsch und Continuatio des abentheurlichen Simplicissimi,* ed. Rolf Tarot (Tübingen: Niemeyer, 1967), 467. Subsequent references to this work are cited in the text using the abbreviation *ST* and page number.

[3] See Watt, *Cheap Print and Popular Piety*, 51.

[4] See Nigel Smith, *Perfection Proclaimed: Language and Literature in English Radical Religion, 1640–1660* (Oxford: Clarendon, 1989), 17.

[5] See C. John Sommerville, *Popular Religion in Restoration England* (Gainesville: U of Florida P, 1977), 33.

[6] See Hans Gerd Rötzer, *Picaro — Landstörtzer — Simplicius: Studien zum niederen Roman in Spanien und Deutschland* (Darmstadt: Wissenschaftliche Buchhandlung, 1972), 100.

[7] See Roger Sharrock, introduction to *The Pilgrim's Progress*, by John Bunyan (Harmondsworth, U.K.: Penguin, 1987), xvi–xvii.

[8] See Frank Baudach, *Planeten der Unschuld — Kinder der Natur: Die Naturstandsutopie in der deutschen und westeuropäischen Literatur des 17. und 18. Jahrhunderts* (Tübingen: Niemeyer, 1993), 47.

[9] Baudach, 47.

[10] Baudach, 47.

[11] See Carl August von Bloedau, *Grimmelshausens Simplicissimus und seine Vorgänger: Beiträge zur Romantechnik des siebzehnten Jahrhunderts* (Berlin: Mayer & Müller, 1908), 36.

[12] Augustinian elements in Grimmelshausen's novel are mentioned throughout the secondary literature, including the following: Dieter Breuer, "Grimmelshausens simplicianische Frömmigkeit: Zum Augustinismus des 17. Jahrhunderts," *Chloe* 2 (1983): 213–52; Friedrich Gaede, *Poetik und Logik: Zu den Grundlagen der literarischen Entwicklung im 17. und 18. Jahrhundert* (Bern: Francke, 1978), 71; Hans Geulen, "'Verwunderungs und Aufhebens werth': Erläuterungen und Bedenken zu Grimmelshausens *Simplicissimus Teutsch*" [special issue: *Grimmelshausen und seine Zeit: Die Vorträge des Münsteraner Symposions zum 300. Todestag des Dichters*, ed. G. Weydt and R. Wimmer], *Daphnis* 5, nos. 2–4 (1976): 209; idem, "Wirklichkeitsbegriff und Realismus in Grimmelshausens *Simplicissimus Teutsch*," *Argenis* 1 (1977): 33; Axel Schmitt, "Intertextuelles Verwirrspiel: Grimmelshausens Simplicianische Schriften im Labyrinth der Sinnkonstitution," *Simpliciana* 15 (1993): 81–82; Peter Triefenbach, *Der Lebenslauf des Simplicius Simplicissimus: Figur–Initiation–Satire* (Stuttgart: Ernst Klett, 1979), 58.

[13] Walter Busch, "Die Lebensbeichte einer Warenseele: Satirische Aspekte der Schermesser-Allegorie in Grimmelshausens *Continuatio*," *Simpliciana* 9 (1987): 58.

[14] Baudach, *Planeten der Unschuld — Kinder der Natur*, 49–50.

[15] Baudach, 50.

[16] Scholte, *Der Simplicissimus und sein Dichter*, 247–48.

[17] "Euer Rede aber sey Ja Ja / Nein Nein / was drüber ist / das ist vom Ubel" (*ST*, 72). Translation: "Your speech should be yes, yes, no, no; whatever is beyond that is wicked."

[18] Gaede draws attention to the need for a complete narrative to answer these questions, whose formal answers without their surrounding context simply do not make sense. Friedrich Gaede, "Das 'Beschreiben' bei Grimmelshausen," *Simpliciana* 12 (1990): 182.

[19] See Günter Rohrbach, *Figur und Charakter: Strukturuntersuchungen an Grimmelshausens "Simplicissimus"* (Bonn: H. Bouvier, 1959), 40.

[20] The critics who read *Simplicissimus* as a Bildungsroman or *Entwicklungsroman* include: Johannes Alt, *Grimmelshausen und der "Simplicissimus"* (Munich: C. H. Beck, 1936); Friedrich Gundolf, "Grimmelshausen und der 'Simplicissimus'" (1923), in *Der Simplicissimusdichter und sein Werk*, ed. G. Weydt (Darmstadt: Wissenschaftliche Buchhandlung, 1969), 111–32; and Melitta Gerhard, "Grimmelshausens 'Simplicissimus' als Entwicklungsroman" (1926), in *Der Simplicissimusdichter und sein Werk*, 133–60.

[21] See Hans Dieter Gebauer, *Grimmelshausens Bauerndarstellung: Literarische Sozialkritik und ihr Publikum* (Marburg: Elwert, 1977), 177–78.

[22] Hubert Gersch, *Geheimpoetik: Die "Continuatio des abentheurlichen Simplicissimi" interpretiert als Grimmelshausens verschlüsselter Kommentar zu seinem Roman* (Tübingen: Niemeyer, 1973), 114–16.

[23] Hans Jakob Christoph von Grimmelshausen, *Der seltzame Springinsfeld*, ed. Franz Günter Sieveke (Tübingen: Niemeyer, 1969), 16, 45, 47. Subsequent references to this work are cited in the text using the abbreviation *SP* and page number.

[24] I am indebted to Terry Llewellyn for drawing my attention to the connection between the reference to wine in *Simplicissimus* and Simplicius's trick in *Springinsfeld*.

4: Introduction to the *Robinsonade*

DANIEL DEFOE'S *ROBINSON CRUSOE* was a great hit when it was first published, and it quickly attracted many imitators. Many subsequent works of realistic adventure fiction consciously use Robinsonade episodes to capitalize on *Crusoe*'s popularity. Through imitation authors build up a specific set of conventions to satisfy reader expectations. Establishing these conventions is an important stage in the evolution of the eighteenth-century novel as a respected and clearly identifiable literary genre. Although Schnabel acknowledges the questionable reputation of *Crusoe* imitations in 1731, Jean-Jacques Rousseau recommends *Robinson Crusoe* as a work of great educational value in 1762. Writers like Joachim Heinrich Campe, Johann Wyss, and Captain Frederick Marryat use the genre as a vehicle for serious pedagogy. In so doing, they give children's adventure novels a seal of approval and pave the way for more fantastical and sensationalistic works.

I propose the following definition of the Robinsonade: a story or an episode within a story where an individual or group of individuals with limited resources try to survive on a desert island. German critics have spent generations defining the Robinsonade, examining the historical usage of the term, and discussing which books should or should not be included in the genre. There are valid arguments in favor of including a wide variety of survival texts in the genre. There are also arguments both for and against applying the term to texts that were written before the word was even invented. I am here using the term as a convenient way of identifying certain universal characteristics in novels that employ a common set of motifs in a similar way.

In the remaining chapters in this book I will discuss *Robinson Crusoe* and Schnabel's *Wunderliche Fata einiger See-Fahrer* because they reflect the development of the Robinsonade genre. The editor in the preface to *Crusoe* does not know quite what sort of a book he is introducing, but a decade later Schnabel's editor figure, Gisander, addresses several different sets of reader expectations in his introduction. Grimmelshausen's *Simplicissimus* also ends with an episode set on a desert island. With a few minor differences — the episode is short and does not concentrate on technological development and innovation to any great extent — Grimmelshausen's desert island plays a role similar to the desert islands in the other two novels. Examining this episode shows that many of the conventions of the Robinsonade do not begin with *Crusoe*. Instead, they are variations of images taken from Christian iconography. The successful adaptation of characteristically Christian images and of the structure of spiritual autobiography within a realistic setting is undoubtedly one reason for the relatively quick acceptance of desert island fiction as constructive reading for the young.

Grimmelshausen, Defoe, and Schnabel use the desert island as the setting for a closed experiment. Because of their isolation on the islands, the various protagonists learn to understand themselves and to read the evidence of God's intervention in their lives. The authors of these texts construct the topography and physical features of the islands so that they possess a spiritual significance or psychological meaning. Characters discover their destiny by interacting with the island landscape, just as Christian comes to understand his own role in God's story by traveling through the scriptural landscape. The use of the Robinsonade motif in these novels differs from the use of the pilgrimage motif in Bunyan's work in one important respect: the destination of the journey in the Robinsonade is not known. Bunyan's pilgrims know where they are traveling, but only divine providence knows how the stories of the castaways in *Crusoe* or the *Wunderliche Fata* will end.

The journeying portions of the Robinsonade tend to be aimless and governed by chance, while the protagonists' psychological and spiritual development usually takes place in a fairly static situation on the island. Despite these differences, the basic premise of the story and its overall structure are very similar to Bunyan's works. Individuals must discover God's plans for them by learning to understand how their own experiences fit into a larger story. Having understood themselves, they are able to retell their life stories using the basic structure of the spiritual autobiography and speaking through a common set of scriptural paradigms.

The journey through the wilderness to the Promised Land is perhaps the most influential of these paradigms. Early modern sea and shipwreck imagery emphasizes the importance of crossing from a state of ignorance and uncertainty to one of living directly under divine rule. Emblems and other references to the island or rock of safety, reached after braving ocean storms or sea tempests, are omnipresent in seventeenth- and eighteenth-century literature. The use of such imagery is linked with the biblical story of Noah and with the parting of the Red Sea during the flight from Egypt. It also appears in the common metaphor of the church as a ship carrying its congregation to heaven, or of the ship of life, as well as in the use of water baptism to represent the subject's death to original sin and entry into the communion of saints.

In Defoe's novel Crusoe fails to understand what God is trying to tell him when he ignores the meaning of his first shipwreck. When he reaches the island after a good ducking, he instinctively and immediately gives thanks to God for his preservation. For those who arrive at the Insel Felsenburg, the experience is similar. Unlike Robinson Crusoe, whose real conversion occurs later in the text, the moment of shipwreck and disaster coincides with the moment of extreme despair and the relinquishing of the self to divine providence that is a crucial component of the pietistic conversion. Captain Wolffgang describes this process in the greatest detail, while many of the protagonists of the life stories in the first volume provide similar, shorter descriptions. Simplicius experiences a moment of near-conversion when he almost drowns in the Rhine; his description of the experience[1] is reminiscent of descriptions of the action of fortune on the life of man. He realizes that he needs God's help to save himself, but when he is actually rescued he forgets. His later shipwreck plays exactly the same role as that experienced by Crusoe and the Felsenburgers. It results in a recognition of the action of providence and of his own status as chosen by God to survive.

The shipwreck and storm images receive a personal application in *Grace Abounding* that clarifies their importance for the protagonists of the Robinsonade. In failing to appreciate the significance of his rescue from drowning, Bunyan also fails to appreciate an event that his contemporaries interpreted as evidence of the positive intervention of divine providence. Later in the text Bunyan uses storm, tempest, and shipwreck metaphors to describe his extreme mental and spiritual instability. Bunyan's use of sea imagery to describe his soul's distress recalls the shipwreck passages of the *Wunderliche Fata* or *Robinson Crusoe*:

> Thus, by the strange and unusual assaults of the tempter, was my Soul, like a broken Vessel, driven, as with the Winds, and tossed. . . . I was but as those that jostle against the Rocks; more broken, scattered, and rent. (*GA*, 58)

His faith overcomes the turbulence of spiritual uncertainty:

> Oh! I cannot now express what then I saw and felt of the steadiness of Jesus Christ, the Rock of Man's Salvation. . . . I saw, indeed, that sin might drive the Soul beyond Christ, even the sin which is unpardon-

able; but woe to him that was so driven, for the word would shut him out. (*GA*, 58)

Bunyan equates certainty, steadiness, and rootedness with his recognition of Christ's role in man's salvation, while motion reflects the spiritual uncertainty and lack of faith that tosses him from one incorrect doctrine to the next. His use of this imagery in connection with his interpretive difficulties during conversion agrees with Timothy Reiss's reference to the frequent early modern use of the image of a difficult sea voyage to refer to the loss and rediscovery of discourse.[2]

An even more thorough application of the image appears in Johann Arndt's influential *Vier Bücher vom Wahren Christenthum*:

> Die *Welt* und *unser elendes Leben* ist nichts anders, denn ein ungestümes Meer; denn gleichwie das Meer nimmer stille ist, sondern allezeit mit Winden und Wellen bewogen wird: Also ist die Welt auch, und unser Leben. . . . Gleichwie auch das Meer ab- und zufleust, und nimmer stille stehet, bald fleussets zurück, bald kömmt es wieder, und ist in perpetuo motu, in steter Bewegung: Also ists mit dem Zeitlichen auch, bald kömmts, bald fährts wieder hin, und ist in stetem Ab- und Zufluß. Und wie des Meers fluxus und refluxus, Ab- und Zufluß, eine verborgene Ursach hat: Also kömmt alle Veränderung des menschlichen Zustandes aus verborgenem Rath GOttes.[3]

> [The world and our miserable lives are nothing more than an unsettled sea; for just as the sea is never still, but is always moved by the wind and the waves, so too are our lives and the world. . . . Just as the sea flows to and fro and never stands still, sometimes flowing backward, sometimes returning, in perpetual motion, so it is with temporal things too — now they come, now they go again, they are in a constant state of ebb and flow. And just as the sea's flux and reflux, ebb and flow, has a hidden cause, so too do all the changes in the human condition come from the hidden guidance of God.]

Arndt's description summarizes the significant elements of shipwreck imagery in the fictional texts under discussion. On the one hand, the stormy sea is an explicit manifestation of the extreme mutability and flux of human life. Because flux and instability occur as a result of the Fall, he associates them with individual sin and with life in the sinful world. On the other hand, this surface unrest is only superficial. The chaotic appearance hides an order powered by an unseen hand, the systematic movement of the tides. In the

Robinsonade the movement through the superficial unrest of the sea to the earthly paradise is a movement from sinfulness toward a deeper understanding of the hidden divine order. Characters move from the realm of fortune to the governance of divine providence.

When the protagonists in the novels recognize the guiding hand of providence, they realize that there is a rational order structuring individual experience. When they know that their experiences fit together logically, they are able to approach their lives systematically — both in terms of physical, civilizing activity and in terms of the literary account, the autobiography. The island becomes an area of settlement and of narrative generation. The earthly paradise, as the rock of physical and spiritual salvation, confirms the chosen nature of the individuals who reach it.

The experience of shipwreck tends to have a common set of meanings in most Robinsonade episodes. The isolation of characters on a desert island also has similar implications throughout the genre. Authors often explicitly compare the individual or small group of individuals living in the island paradise with Adam and Eve. The main characters are revisiting or reenacting the origins of the human race. If their efforts are successful, the civilization they found reverses the fall of man. It is a purified society based on virtue and shared social norms. Just as the island's inhabitants become representative of a wider humanity, the island itself is a microcosm of the wider world. Its varied landscape contains many natural resources and topographical features. Despite the island's spatial limitations, the variety in the landscape allows its inhabitants to perform many different activities, from fishing and sailing to hunting, herding, and tilling the soil. The emphasis on the island as a paradise means that the characters who learn to live within the landscape are often very conscious of it as a created space, an element in God's creation.

The island is isolated. Its isolation allows its inhabitants to escape from the corrupt world. They are often the only ones who have survived a shipwreck situation. This isolation has two consequences, one spiritual and the other psychological. From a religious viewpoint — as a genre that is frequently heavily didactic, the Robinsonade most often retains a religious element — the characters on the island are a chosen people. They alone have been saved while others perished; they alone will form the basis of this new civilization in the Promised Land. The island landscape exists for them in the sense that they have been placed on it by God. Everything that happens upon it is a sign of a greater divine plan. Providence intervenes directly in the lives of the people on the island. As a chosen people, they must recognize this and act in a way that will fulfill the destiny of the island.

Even if the spiritual element were entirely absent from the Robinsonade situation, the psychological aspect would still remain relevant. The isolated individual or social group has been put on the island for a reason — by the author of the text, if not by God. The author treats the isolated, closed landscape of the island almost as a scientific experiment in order to examine how its inhabitants respond to their isolation in the wilderness. Because the island appears in a book, only specific bits of it are important. The author tells his readers about the landscape only insofar as it has meaning. The presence of humans and their stories provides it with significance. The landscape becomes a reflection of the characters as they change it, name it, and transform the wilderness that surrounds them. Although it appears empirically realistic, the island landscape is, in fact, as full of meaning as the allegorical landscape through which Christian travels in *The Pilgrim's Progress*. It is the vehicle by means of which readers can learn to understand the characters and characters can learn to better understand themselves.

There is one more aspect of the desert island as an earthly paradise that is important in relation to language and storytelling. In my introductory chapter I referred to the basic pattern of all of these texts (roughly "fall — wandering through the wilderness of the world — baptism — conversion through grace — salvation") as the pattern of the Old and New Testaments read as a whole. The plot of each text is clearly *not* limited to a linear cause-and-effect chronology. Forward-looking prophecies and the presence of retrospective narrators in the works show that the story can be read from different perspectives. It exists independently of the normal constraints of time because it can be read forward, backward, and chronologically as it unfolds. The plot of these texts is preordained according to a universal framework and must, in a sense, be discovered by the characters who journey through it.

The protagonists believe in the existence of a single, divinely inspired plan that explains all human experience and directs all of creation. If the sinful world is depicted as an area of disrupted and problematic communication, the regenerate world appears as an area of harmonious discourse. Learning to speak God's language and understand His story reverses the communication difficulties that are the result of original sin and reinstates the direct relation between word and meaning, signifier and signified.[4] Individual characters in the earthly paradise are able to communicate with God and to understand why their experiences occur and what they mean.

Because God's story is so comprehensive, understanding the relationship between personal experiences and this universal story also means understanding the world. Learning to read the divine narrative means learning to read both personal experience and the natural realm in terms of their spiritual significance. Once characters are able to understand the empirical world, they learn to make use of the objects in their environments. The things they collect and scavenge are God-given tools to bring about the fulfillment of the island's destiny and that of its characters. Nineteenth-century Robinsonade episodes optimistically describe their characters' abilities to use these tools as evidence of God's benevolence in creating the world expressly for human use. Earlier texts make a connection with the pure, uncorrupted language that existed in paradise. They tend to see this insight into the nature of material things as evidence that characters have overcome their worldly corruption.

The concept of pure signification harks back to Adam naming the animals in Genesis. Johann Arndt describes Adam's command of language as follows:

> Welche Merckzeichen und Signatur Adam aus eingeschaffener Weißheit alle wohl verstanden; nemlich die Physiognomiam aller lebendigen Thiere, daraus er ihre eingepflanzte Art, Natur und Eigenschaft erkannt und dieselbe ihrer unterschiedliche Art nach mit ihrem eigentlichen natürlichen Namen genennet, welcher Name eines ieden Thiers Art, Natur und Eigenschaft in sich begriffen hat.[5]

> [Because of his inherent wisdom, Adam understood all these characteristics and signatures, namely, the physiognomy of all living creatures. From this he recognized their implanted type, nature, and quality and named each according to its type with its own natural name; each name contained within itself an understanding of each creature's type, nature, and quality.]

Thomas Browne, too, writes that the divine language is completely unified and fully expresses the nature of what it signifies:

> The finger of God hath left an inscription upon all his works, not graphicall or composed of letters, but of their severall formes, constitutions, parts, and operations, which aptly joyned together doe make one word that doth express their natures. By these Letters God cals the

Starres by their names, and by this Alphabet *Adam* assigned to every creature a name peculiar to its Nature.[6]

George Fox, the founder of the Society of Friends, moves beyond Arndt and Browne in describing the Adamic state as one that the enlightened individual may regain or even transcend:

> I knew nothing but pureness, and innocency, and righteousness, being renewed up into the image of God by Christ Jesus, so that I say I was come up to the state of Adam which he was in before he fell. The creation was opened to me, and it was showed me how all things had their names given them according to their nature and virtue. And I was at a stand in my mind whether I should practise physic for the good of mankind, seeing the nature and virtues of the creatures were so opened to me by the Lord.[7]

Fox describes a practical mastery of the medicinal arts as a result of the insight provided by his enlightenment. The concept of the Adamic language and the return to the Adamic state implies a mastery of the empirical world that is the result of understanding the true nature and significance of material objects. Perfecting the protagonist's ability to perceive, understand, and interpret his or her natural environment accompanies the perfected ability to communicate with God and with virtuous fellow humans.

In Baroque thought the concept of the Adamic language appears in association with emblematics,[8] religious mysticism, the early study of linguistics, and even science and natural history.[9] In popular seventeenth- and eighteenth-century religious and hermetic literature, the search for the language of Adam frequently does not focus on an actual grammatical language but rather on restoring the ability to read the divinely appointed meaning of signs, whether in the form of words or objects. The Adamic language thus has a specific connection with allegoresis and Jakob Böhme's doctrine of the signatures,[10] as well as with the more general ability to generate language whose meaning is pure, true, and complete.

The protagonists in these works show that they have reversed the effects of the Fall on language in different ways. Simplicius learns to read the Book of Nature correctly, while Crusoe and the inhabitants of Felsenburg master many different arts. As in many utopias, this indicates a return to some form of universal knowledge, in this case one based on man's ability to master his surroundings by understanding them rationally. Crusoe and Simplicius reveal their comprehension of multiple languages, while Crusoe and Albertus Julius organize societies governed directly by natural and divine law. Telling each individual story from the viewpoint of the enlightened narrator serves as the ultimate confirmation of the mastery of the universal language. In the three Robinsonade episodes, the return to the Adamic language is intimately connected with the return to a harmonious natural state. It is a return to Adam's mastery over the Garden of Eden in the form of the island paradise. The earthly paradise is a location, but it is also a blessed spiritual state, an area that leads to the generation of stories.

Notes

[1] "So spielte dennoch der Strom mit mir wie mit einem Ballen / in dem er mich bald über-bald undersich in Grund warf" (*ST,* 320). Translation: "The current played with me as with a ball; sometimes it threw me up, sometimes under itself toward the bottom."

[2] Timothy J. Reiss, *The Discourse of Modernism* (Ithaca, NY: Cornell UP, 1982), 153.

[3] Johann Arnd[t], *Vier Bücher vom Wahren Christenthum,* ed. D. Joachim Langen (Halle: Verlag des Wäysenhauses, 1734), 940–41.

[4] See Reiss, *The Discourse of Modernism,* 76–77.

[5] Arndt, *Vier Bücher vom Wahren Christenthum,* 945–46.

[6] Thomas Browne, *Religio Medici* (1643; reprint, Menston, U.K.: Scolar, 1970, 138.

[7] George Fox, *The Journal of George Fox,* ed. John L. Nickalls (Cambridge: Cambridge UP, 1952), 27.

[8] See Dietrich Walter Jöns, *Das "Sinnen-Bild": Studien zur allegorischen Bildlichkeit bei Andreas Gryphius* (Stuttgart: Metzler, 1966), 6–11. According to Jöns, the mystical sense and symbolic language of the Bible connect it with emblems and hieroglyphs. According to Renaissance Neoplatonic thought, they are examples of a hidden, ancient, universal writing.

[9] See Hans Blumenberg, *Die Lesbarkeit der Welt* (Frankfurt am Main: Suhrkamp, 1981), 87.

[10] See Nigel Smith, ed., *A Collection of Ranter Writings from the Seventeenth Century* (London: Junction, 1983), 30–31; see also Smith, *Perfection Proclaimed,* 279–80.

5: Defoe's *Robinson Crusoe*

DANIEL DEFOE'S *ROBINSON CRUSOE* has been hailed as the first English novel. It certainly was one of the most influential among the early English novels, and it was directly responsible for creating the genre of the desert island novel, or Robinsonade. Secondary criticism usually treats *Robinson Crusoe* in one of two ways. Critics sometimes look from *Crusoe* forward. They discover in *Crusoe* the seeds of the English social novel, with its emphasis on empirical reality, verisimilitude, and detailed observation. They also describe the influence of Enlightenment philosophical and economic thought on Defoe's work. A second group of critics aligns itself with G. A. Starr and J. Paul Hunter. They tend to look from Crusoe backward to identify the dominant influences on the themes and structure of Defoe's novel.

Crusoe appears sandwiched between the genres of religious writing popular in the seventeenth century — especially the spiritual autobiography — and the well-developed novels of the mid and late eighteenth century. Although it is an important transitional work because of its focus on individual psychology and empirical detail, it also includes a great deal of material that is explicitly religious. The spiritual aspect of the text differs from Bunyan's work in two important respects: reason is far more important in this text and the story is primarily fictional rather than allegorical, its editor's claims notwithstanding.

Defoe's novel is far more optimistic than any of the other works under discussion. Bunyan, Grimmelshausen, and even Schnabel describe the world as senseless and chaotic as a result of its distance from God. The task of the individual protagonists is to discover or develop their understanding of how God shows Himself in creation by learning to read the signs around them, their experiences, and the Bible. This process and its results remain fraught with tension, which partially explains why the works have difficulty achieving closure.

The source of Defoe's optimism lies in the English Enlightenment. God appears in the text in Crusoe's descriptions of his conversion experience and in his struggle to understand why he has been placed on the island. At the same time, however, Crusoe displays a faith in reason and rational organization that makes it the very principle of all existence, whether natural or supernatural. He describes how both divine providence[1] and the devil (*RC*, 155) follow logical paths in assisting or tempting humans. The battle between elect and reprobate language occurs within Crusoe himself, in the tension between Crusoe's naïve, emotional reactions to his experiences and his rational reflections on their significance. Crusoe's rational and reflecting voice gains authority as the text progresses. His rational abilities permit him to develop and civilize the island, to work in concert with providence, and to successfully understand and make his way through the outside world once he has left the island.

The complete dominance of reason in Crusoe's world is extraordinary when compared with those presented by the other authors. The worlds Bunyan and Grimmelshausen depict are so corrupt that they follow no rules. The only way the main characters can hope to escape persecution and achieve peace and rest is to leave worldly life entirely. Even in Schnabel's *Wunderliche Fata* (which was written after *Crusoe*), reason only has power within the confines of the island and supernatural forces do not always follow the rules of logic and cause and effect. Crusoe's island is an earthly paradise where he finds salvation, but it is also a laboratory within which he can dissect every aspect of human life and technology and figure out how it all works. He learns to understand his experiences and to think in a rational way. Once he has confirmed these insights by telling his story to a progressively widening audience, he is free to leave the island and seek adventures in the world at large. His search may be spiritual, but his story does not end in any transcendent salvation. Crusoe's world is inherently rational, created by a rational God for a rational man. Paradoxically, it is also a fictional world.

In order to gain control over his fate, Crusoe must learn to see his experiences in terms of the bigger picture. God is directing his experiences, but Crusoe's perspective is limited and he has difficulty understanding what his story means and where it will end. Crusoe is alone throughout the better part of his story, so most of the examples of elect and reprobate language spring from within Crusoe himself. At the beginning of the story, however, Defoe provides two examples of characters who already possess the broader and more comprehensive understanding that Crusoe seeks throughout the novel.

Early in the novel Crusoe's father warns him against his restlessness and his desire to travel. Providence has situated Crusoe comfortably in the middle station of life, and his wish to leave it is contrary to reason. Although

Crusoe rejects his surroundings and the moderate and ordered lifestyle of his father, he does not know why. He is unable to name or define his desire. Crusoe's actions display the limited perspective and resulting aimlessness and lack of control that Defoe represents as man's fallen and natural state. His father's superior understanding is the product of worldly experience and religious knowledge. He knows how the world works, so he can tell where his son is heading.

The sea captain confirms Crusoe's father's predictions of disaster for his irrational son. Like Crusoe's father, the captain's situation in life is the one to which providence has called him, and he recognizes that God has a specific plan in mind for each person. He understands the moral significance of his experiences on the sea, and he is able to make connections between personal experience and the lessons taught in the Bible. When he hears about Crusoe's disastrous experiences, he compares Crusoe's story with Jonah's and declares that God's hand is raised against the young man (*RC*, 15). Both characters are able to make their predictions because they believe that God acts in a rational and explicable way. They only need to read the signs in a present situation to predict how a story will end in the future.

While he is on his desert island, Crusoe spends a great deal of time thinking about how to understand his situation. Once he draws up a balance sheet to contrast the positive and negative interpretations of his condition, he discovers how to control and stabilize his own mental state. Logical reflection helps him to understand the broader parameters of his story and God's purpose in causing certain events.

The balance sheet is weighted toward the positive side of the interpretation, which identifies God as the preserver of Crusoe's life and the provider of whatever material comforts he possesses. More importantly, it reflects the self-awareness and the self-conscious exercise of reason that allow Crusoe to master himself and his environment. By means of the balance sheet Crusoe gives his reflecting, reasoning self a mark of moral approval ("Good") that continues throughout the text. In a similar fashion, it is possible to summarize the value of the balance sheet in establishing the authority of Crusoe's rational voice. After examining his different interpretations of his experiences, Crusoe concludes that there is a good and correct way for him to react to his situation:

Bad Reactions	Good Reactions
• Despair because of physical need or physical situation	• Thankfulness at physical preservation
• Immediate and uncontrolled responses to experience; action without reflection	• Reflection; exercise of rational capabilities; self-conscious counsel; interior dialogue
• Irrational inability to see ends/results of activities or circumstances	• Rational ability to predict cause and effect; ability to organize activity (work or writing) methodically, according to its meaning or purpose
• Attributing events to chance or chaos	• Order; ability to see reason in experience, particularly in relation to divine providence
• Knowledge limited to empirical perception and reaction to phenomena in the empirical world; "act[ing] like a meer Brute from the Principles of Nature, and by the Dictates of common Sense only" (*RC*, 88)	• Reflecting on experiences and imagining what could have happened, which leads to greater knowledge of God's plan and results in appreciation and thanksgiving even for hardships because they have a purpose when looked at in the greater context

Crusoe assigns himself three identities in the balance sheet. The voice of Crusoe as the writer of the sheet dominates the voice of the evil side and the voice of the good side. He organizes and reviews the positions of the good and bad voices in relation to each other. Because the balance sheet uses a rational format to organize Crusoe's emotions, the reflective voice of the good side is most congenial to Crusoe as the writer of the sheet. Although the sheet tends to recognize the negative interpretations of his situation, it affirms the positive interpretations. This mirrors the approving relationship between the narrating Crusoe and the reflecting, rational Crusoe on the island. The former reflects on and organizes the whole of his experience into a comprehensive narrative, while the latter orders his experience as he develops spiritually.

By means of the balance sheet Crusoe is able to recognize the coexistence of possible interpretations of the same situation.[2] Writing down the summary stabilizes Crusoe's alternating mental states so that he can view both simultaneously. For the first time in the text he attains an uninterrupted perspective and recognizes the presence of alternative states of his own mind. The content of the sheet is less important than the fact that it is drawn up. It represents Crusoe's first successful attempt to order his experience and provides a model for how to deal with subsequent mental confusion. Throughout his story it is necessary for Crusoe to state the views of the naïve, experiencing voice in order to transcend their shortcomings.

In response to the balance sheet, Crusoe states the rule that he uses whenever he tries to understand his personal experiences. According to what I will call his law of contraries, Crusoe must use his imagination to consider the positive aspects of each experience. He contrasts them with what might have been a worst-case scenario in order to understand what the real value and purpose of the experience might be:

> There was scarce any Condition in the World so miserable, but there was something *Negative* or something *Positive* to be thankful for in it; and let this stand as a Direction from the Experience of the most miserable of all Conditions in this World, that we may always find in it something to comfort our selves from, and to set in the Description of Good and Evil, on the Credit Side of the Accompt. (*RC*, 67)

Crusoe later remarks that "we never see the true State of our Condition, till it is illustrated to us by its Contraries; nor know how to value what we enjoy, but by the want of it" (*RC*, 139). The most effective way for Crusoe to learn to appreciate the good side of his situation is to experience a state that is worse, but he can also learn to be thankful for his lot by envisioning the alternative possibilities in his head. Experience may be a good teacher, but in learning how to think logically and avoid making mistakes Crusoe also learns that the lessons taught by the imagination are less painful.

The way Crusoe approaches events in his life is the same as the way readers interpret the events in a book. They ask themselves questions like the following: What happened? What could have happened instead? What did the author intend by making the event happen the way it did? According to Crusoe, God is the author who decides what will happen to him. Crusoe must learn to view his life as a story and to ask himself questions about its author's hidden intentions. To succeed in answering these questions, he must combine his ability to make logical deductions with his ability to imagine alternative situations and to envision the effects of his actions.

Crusoe eventually arrives at a definitive interpretation of his experiences and learns to tell his story correctly, but the path to understanding is fraught with difficulties. Before reaching the island, his limited perspective does not move beyond a concern about his physical welfare. While he is on the island, he strives to reach a higher understanding of his position in the world, but his mental instability continually returns him to the same blind concern for his own material preservation.

Crusoe's ignorance at the beginning of the story causes his willful disobedience. The explicit rejection of religion and duty (*RC,* 131) that accompanies his rejection of parental authority is only a sign of his fundamental corruption. Crusoe's basic inclination toward disobedience is part of his fallen nature, as is the narrow perspective that confines his understanding to the material realm. Crusoe's ability to understand his situation remains flawed throughout his travels — even during his captivity in Sallee. Crusoe perceives the literal fulfillment of his father's prophecy as the fulfillment of a curse. His mistaken reading excludes any spiritual element. He does not draw any parallels between his physical state of captivity and his spiritual state despite the obvious significance of the Moorish episode. Despite references to the affection that exists between them, his relationship with Xury is based solely on physical need and cooperation.

When Crusoe looks back on the episode, he realizes it only foreshadows his future tribulations (*RC,* 19). Crusoe's mistaken reading is based on his failure to apply the law of contraries. He fails to set his experience within a broader context, to realize that his situation could indeed be worse, and to be thankful that it is not. He does not learn to appreciate the positive aspects of his situation because he does not tell himself the story of what did *not* happen to him. In fact, Crusoe's failure to move beyond purely utilitarian principles to any form of religious reflection causes him to give up Xury, which leads to his need for slaves on his plantation, which in turn leads to his shipwreck on the island. Like Simplicius, his preoccupation with the material world causes him to move restlessly from place to place and from one source of profit to another. It is ultimately responsible for his presence on the island.

Although Crusoe's interpretive ability and knowledge develop during his sojourn on the island, he continues to find it difficult to reconcile his individual desires with the divine plan until almost the conclusion of his stay. As his first attempt at boat-making illustrates, immoderate desire tends to cloud his judgment. Because he does not stop to observe his surroundings carefully and does not plan what he is going to do, he makes a boat so large that he cannot move it. It thus becomes a memorial to his folly.[3] Although Crusoe realizes that he has made a mistake, he does not extrapolate further to realize that the basic imbalance between desire and forethought caused his miscalculation. Disasters occur when he acts out of rashness and ignorance. He is so eager to satisfy his desires that he fails to systematically plan the series of actions that will result in their gratification (*RC*, 138).

When Crusoe makes his ill-fated attempt to take a boat to the other side of the island, the currents almost sweep him out to sea. His meeting with Poll the parrot on the way home underlines the fact that he has been lost both physically and spiritually in the course of the episode. His encounter with the parrot, who seems to speak with his own disembodied voice, shows that in his immoderate desire to escape he has ignored the rational and spiritual portion of his personality. Poll literally appears as the voice of conscience. He does not bemoan Crusoe's presence on the island, as he has been taught.[4] Instead, his words focus on Crusoe's mistaken absence: "Where are you? Where have you been?" (*RC*, 142). Crusoe's confused and frightened reaction to the parrot's appearance shows that he has reverted to responding naïvely to appearances. He has temporarily lost his ability to reason because he allowed his actions to be determined by passion.

Crusoe's contact with the savages reflects even more clearly the difficulty of maintaining his state of interpretive competence. Seeing the footprint throws him into a state of confusion. His memory and his interpretive abilities become wild and disordered. The realization that the cannibals were probably on the island during his previous experiences causes him to reinterpret his memories (*RC*, 196–97). He can no longer trust even his basic sensory perceptions and linguistic categories. His first home, which he once described in cozily domestic language,[5] is now rendered in purely military terms.[6] Crusoe's confused mind makes him think natural objects are men. His frightened imagination substitutes its own visions for his accustomed systematic, rational observation, and his confusion obliterates the memory of his arrival at home.

Even when Crusoe has regained his composure, his fear interferes with the physical improvements he intends for his settlement. He gives up plans to invent a method of brewing beer in favor of defending himself. It is only after prolonged reflection that he even forms a hypothesis regarding the origin of the print. He manages to resign himself to the situation only temporarily by reading comforting passages from Scripture. The mere presence of the savages reawakens his irrational desire for escape from the island, which he associates with his original sin of wandering away from his father (*RC*, 194–95). Ironically and illogically, his plan is to escape to the mainland, where the savages live.

Crusoe describes how reason teaches him to understand the significance of his past experiences and how to respond correctly to his environment, yet he also indicates that it is dangerous to rely solely on reason without religion. During his conversion Crusoe's observations of the natural world lead him to reflect on God as its creator. He moves from this thought to recognize the possibility that God has not merely created the empirical world but also guides and sustains it. This is a recognition of the existence of divine providence.

The speculation becomes problematic for Crusoe when he realizes that God, as the controller of all earthly events, has sanctioned — even caused — his plight. This realization results in a divided state beyond which he cannot move. On the one hand, he bemoans his situation, questioning God's actions in a way that his more enlightened conscience finds blasphemous. On the other hand, when his conscience rebukes him, he shows for the first time that he is beginning to acknowledge his own sinful and ignorant nature. Until Crusoe begins to read the Bible and gains repentance through divine grace, he is unable to move beyond this state. He cannot overcome the silence and the rift between his two selves through his own efforts. Logic can only bring Crusoe to a certain point in his effort to understand who he is and why things happen to him. He must experience the same imputed righteousness as Bunyan in *Grace Abounding* in order to recognize the role God plays in structuring his life story and directing his experiences. Without understanding the importance of the events described in the Bible, it is hopeless for him to try to understand his own story.

Although Crusoe frequently makes mistakes, on the whole there is a progressive development in his ability to understand the meaning of events and to tell his story in a way that reflects this meaning. The combined use of reason and his natural imagination enables him to imitate the divine activities of creating and ordering the world. Whether he is making a boat or contemplating the source of his surroundings, Crusoe must proceed from observing individual, empirical objects to understanding the rational principle that governs their nature. His work consists in applying these mathematical and mechanical principles to raw objects. His insight into the divinely appointed meaning of his experiences enables him to organize his existence as a whole.

He develops a system of living that reflects this insight into the reasons and the providential aims that motivate his experiences. His ingenuity is the creative force that motivates him to develop new projects and extend the borders of his microcosmic civilization.

Crusoe's experience of religious conversion is a watershed in the narrative because it signals a change in the way he reads his surroundings and uses language. When he first begins to read, he has little trouble understanding the Bible, but he has difficulty in correctly applying its lessons to his own experience. He naïvely thinks that a passage concerning deliverance means a literal, physical deliverance from his situation on the island. He first transcends this naïve reading by realizing that the meaning of the passage could be relative. It may mean his deliverance from the affliction of sickness instead of his deliverance from the island. A given passage can be applied to a variety of different situations. Only by examining his different experiences in context and comparing them with each other and with what could have happened can Crusoe understand how incidents from the Bible apply to his situation. He must stop reading literally and begin reading spiritually, but he must also develop his understanding of his own situation (*RC,* 96) in order to understand Scripture correctly.

As a result of his conversion, Crusoe learns to interpret the passage concerning deliverance in a different way (*RC,* 97). He begins to hope for a deliverance that is a spiritual deliverance from his guilt rather than a physical or literal escape from the island. His recognition that through sin he has become marooned spiritually, without the power to free himself or to assist himself in any way, eclipses his sense of material isolation. For much of the remainder of the story Crusoe finds it imperative to overcome his spiritual difficulties before he can achieve physical ease and comfort. He has difficulty maintaining his faith because he has problems in evaluating his experiences and recognizing his own weakness, not because he has failed to understand the actual text of the Bible.

As is the case in the other works, the experience of conversion alters Crusoe's command of language and changes how he reads and describes his experiences. Fear and sickness lead to Crusoe's initial prayers. At first he is ignorant and lacks a religious vocabulary (*RC,* 87). He has recourse to set forms and simply repeats *"Lord pity me, Lord have Mercy upon me"* (*RC,* 87). When he begins to read the Bible systematically, he develops the sense of his own sinfulness that is a necessary precondition for conversion. His reading shows Crusoe that Christ is his savior. His grace causes Crusoe's repentance and hope. This revelation first provides Crusoe with words for prayer. He learns to use the words from the Bible in a personalized fashion to describe his experiences. Crusoe claims that this kind of prayer is authentic because a God-given hope, based on the teachings of the Bible, informs his understanding of his condition (*RC,* 96). The connection with the Bible reassures him that God will listen to him. Crusoe must develop his ability to articulate the meaning of his experiences. He describes repeated attempts to tell his story throughout the text, but it is not until after his conversion that he begins to tell it correctly.

Following his religious awakening, Crusoe's reflections on the successive anniversaries of his landing become important exercises of memory and benchmarks of his spiritual development. Crusoe's memory of these events is more than mere remembrance. He constantly reenacts events in his mind and repeats them in his imagination. Experiences that resemble past events reawaken his memory,[7] and he reinterprets these events in light of subsequent developments. Crusoe honors the first anniversary of his arrival on the island with a solemn fast of repentance. He acknowledges that his presence on the island is a form of divine punishment and prays for mercy. He spends his second anniversary giving humble thanks for God's assistance. He is aware of the dangers of religious reflection not grounded in feeling and experience. After being tempted to give thanks for being placed on the island in the first place, he denounces his own near fall into religious hypocrisy. Crusoe is particularly grateful for the gift of repentance and the way God has dispelled his former ignorance concerning his spiritual situation.

Crusoe's positive assessment continues on his fourth anniversary when, after telling himself his story from a different perspective (*RC,* 128), he reflects on some of the positive aspects of his situation — such as his removal from worldly wickedness and worldly rivalries — and becomes sincerely thankful. His utilitarian ethic precludes competition, avarice, and the other negative aspects of civilization represented by money;[8] providence has allowed him to satisfy his material needs. As on other occasions, he considers the negative possibilities of the shipwreck. He contrasts scenes of imagined distress with an optimistic assessment of his situation and present achievements. He provides a list of his previous iniquities and considers that his present state of comfort is evidence that God may indeed have accepted his repentance. This review, occurring two years after his near fall into false piety, brings about a true thankfulness for his condition. If God had punished him the way he deserved, his situation would be much worse. Crusoe is still not happy that he lives alone on the island, but he is very thankful that he has not suffered any greater evils. From this perspective his position on the island is a positive one.

As a result of his anniversary remembrances, Crusoe comes to perceive his life on the island as a series of miracles (*RC*, 132). His experiences reflect the continuous operation of a merciful providence. The coincidence of remarkable dates in his life strengthens his impression that some external force is actually structuring his experiences so that they reveal the greatest possible degree of meaning. The date that he left his father and entered into the spiritual captivity of sin is the same as that on which the Moors took him captive. The date on which he escaped the wreck is the same as that on which he escaped from Moorish captivity. The date of his physical birth is the date of his rebirth as an island castaway. Crusoe's experiences in the physical, empirical world are signs that foreshadow important spiritual events. Both realms are systematically connected because both demonstrate the existence of a divine order. The verifiable, chronological pattern is mathematical proof that God has intervened directly in Crusoe's life. The coincidence of dates is so great that it is obvious that some external force — providence in the fictional account but the novel's author in reality — is structuring his experiences in order to make them appear significant.

It is not enough for Crusoe simply to learn to read the Bible and understand the role of providence in his experiences. In order to verify his insights, he must share them with other people. He does not truly understand his religion until he tries to explain it to Friday. The scene again emphasizes the limitations of natural religion[9] and of unassisted human knowledge. Friday's god, Benamuckee, is a mere creator god. He is old (*RC*, 216), not eternal, and lives within time and space. His home lies just beyond the area familiar to Friday, and he does not intervene in human affairs apart from giving advice to those who visit him in the mountains. Crusoe tries to wrest religious authority from Friday's tribal priests by introducing him to prayer and describing God's power to affect the life of the individual. By attributing possible evil powers to Benamuckee, however, thereby broaching the problem of theodicy, Crusoe manages to embroil himself in difficulties involving logic.

Defoe describes a hierarchy in which divine knowledge assumes the uppermost place and Friday's natural knowledge the lowest. Crusoe's partial understanding appears somewhere in the middle. Embarrassed, Crusoe readily discontinues the argument rather than hazarding a nonscriptural guess as to God's intentions with respect to the devil. This is a positive acknowledgement to God and the reader, if not to Friday, of his own limited understanding. He displays self-awareness and humility because he does not try to manipulate a theology he does not understand to satisfy the demands of human reason. Crusoe prays for assistance and manages to resolve the question by telling Friday the whole story of creation, including the role of the devil and the importance of redemption through Christ.

The scene demonstrates the idea that Scripture has a voice of its own. Crusoe claims that the creed that he and Friday develop on the island springs directly from their reading of the Bible, a text that is plain and easy to understand (*RC,* 221). Simply reading the Bible is enough to teach Crusoe to seek repentance. Later he demonstrates that his reading has given him enough knowledge to convert Friday (*RC,* 221). The power of the text helps Crusoe and Friday to arrive at a correct understanding. Crusoe claims that God's spirit instructs them and makes them obey the lessons they learn from the stories they read (*RC,* 221).

Like the hermit instructing Simplicius, Crusoe discovers that in order to help Friday understand religion, he must tell him the *whole* story, beginning with Lucifer's rebellion and the fallen angels. This is the only way to explain the devil's battle for human souls and Christ's role as Friday's savior. The comprehensive nature of this complete narrative, which embraces all of creation, leaves no place for alternative possibilities or questions. As an entire system, it precludes the existence of any autonomous discourse and possesses its own inherent logic and causality. Crusoe's ability to understand and tell this story is the necessary precursor to his being able to tell his own story.

Robinson Crusoe spends much of his time in a state of complete isolation — in fact, more than any of the characters in the other texts. He does not manage to invent ink. Apart from his journal and a few preliminary reports penned prior to his island adventure, he does not begin to tell his story to others until almost the end of the book. To those who arrive at the island, however, Crusoe's experiences do not require any form of written documentation. The settlement provides all the necessary evidence of his past accomplishments and makes it clear that Crusoe's story reaches a positive conclusion. In order to reintegrate himself into society, Crusoe must ensure that the authority and control he has established on the island extends to the outside world. This occurs through a process of showing and telling similar to the tour of the island in Schnabel's text. This process is successful. When Crusoe's fellows accept his way of life as the dominant system for the island's civilization, they allow Crusoe's authority to extend beyond his isolated self.

Crusoe is able to promote his own authority successfully for two reasons. In practical terms he possesses a comprehensive overview of the topography of the island and an exhaustive knowledge of the technical and mechanical activities necessary to exist successfully within this environment. These practical achievements mean that he can observe the activities of the intruders unseen. His superior knowledge allows him to manipulate their perceptions with relative ease. His spiritual competence matches his technical achievements. Crusoe recognizes the many connections between his own personal story, which continually displays the direct intervention of divine providence, and the story he reads in the Bible. Because of this, he has confidence in the legitimacy of his own organizational system and in how he understands his situation. By the time Friday arrives, Crusoe is sure that he has been put on the island for a reason and that he is living directly under the governance of God. His way of life represents the victory of reason over the irrational. Crusoe's confidence appears in his storytelling and writing. His authority is the basis of the sympathetic relationship between himself and his reasonable audience.

In order to return to civilization, Crusoe must expand his understanding of God's role in his life so that his story can include a series of potentially threatening rival forces, namely, the cannibals, the Spaniards, and the mutineers. He capitalizes on the confusion and despair of others in order to direct their roles in the plot of his life. Saving Friday's soul confirms Crusoe's status as a chosen instrument of providence. Crusoe cannot free himself from the threat the savages pose merely by means of his weapons and fortifications, but he succeeds in reestablishing his own mental stability by demonstrating that his rational, civilized way of life is indeed superior to that of the savages. Because of Friday's presence, the settlement assumes the character of a family home. It becomes an earthly paradise rather than a place of exile (*RC,* 220).

During the next stage in the development of the island, Crusoe rescues Friday's father and the Spaniard. The island is transformed from the family home of a patriarchal civilization to a small kingdom, with Crusoe as its ruler. He hosts a feast for Friday's father and the Spaniard to confirm his return to civilization in a role of authority. He once considered that his father might have the fatted calf killed for him upon his return home. Now, as the king of his domain, Crusoe has a goat killed to welcome his new subjects. Crusoe's superior knowledge is visible during the entire rescue attempt, in particular the scene in which Crusoe and Friday view the savages from the bushes.

In comments throughout the novel, Crusoe emphasizes the threat that the rival religion of the bloodthirsty and inhuman Catholic Spaniards poses to his own English Protestant belief (*RC,* 172). The Spaniard dispels this threat when he acknowledges Crusoe's divinely sanctioned role in saving him. The relationship between Friday and his father neutralizes the threat that the presence of another savage poses. Because he is better integrated into Crusoe's civilization, Friday acts as Crusoe's interpreter, not the other white man. The hierarchy of authority on the island thus appears as follows:

1. God.
2. Crusoe as the interpreter of the aims of divine providence.
3. Friday as follower of Crusoe's interpretations.
4. Friday's father and the Spaniard as secondary followers.

Crusoe recognizes that if he assists the Spaniards in escaping to the island and returning to civilization, their religion and their social institutions will pose a significant threat to his own. Crusoe would rather be eaten by cannibals than have his religion and his autonomy destroyed by the merciless claws of Catholicism. The Spaniard demonstrates that he is trustworthy, however, by refusing to disrupt the agricultural system that Crusoe has developed on the island. He demonstrates the rational forethought that is the foundation of Crusoe's success by very reasonably suggesting that they *first* cultivate more land and *then* rescue his companions. The Spaniards accept Crusoe's authority, and in the sequel they show themselves to be positive and moral, even if they do not always share the sheer ingenuity of the English mutineers.

Crusoe finds his interactions with his countrymen even more satisfying, albeit more challenging, than saving the Spaniard and Friday's father. Through these interactions the island society develops further. As in his other encounters, Crusoe's language reflects the change. He describes his settlement using imperialistic and bureaucratic terminology. His home becomes the palace of the governor. His own identity changes to reflect his dual role as master and hands-on laborer in the island civilization. The contact with the English is a crucial step in his reintegration into his own civilization. He displays his ability to counteract not only the simple savagery that exists in man but also the more subtle and deceptive sinfulness of worldly, civilized society.

The nationality of the sailors is particularly important. Unlike the Spaniards and the savages, the English sailors share Crusoe's language and his religious and cultural background. The good sailors — particularly the English captain — display an almost instant appreciation of the significance of Crusoe's story because of this shared language. The mutineers do not participate in an honest narrative exchange. Crusoe initially refuses to reveal his identity to them, but he is careful to leave them a copy of his narrative and a bag of peas when he departs. Both objects will sow the seeds of a new society. Crusoe himself was a reprobate when shipwrecked on the island, and in his autobiography he shows his readers how they must learn to think in order to survive.

During his first encounter with the sailors, Crusoe benefits from his superior knowledge. He explicitly describes his comprehensive perspective when he looks at the mutineers' bound victims. He compares their despair with his own former ignorance concerning the hidden intervention of providence. The prisoners' ignorance is a sign of man's general lack of awareness of God's hidden purposes. The knowledge Crusoe derives from correct observation reinforces his authority. By revealing that he has seen the mutineers threatening to kill the captain, he gives the impression that he possesses superhuman omniscience. In response, the captain exclaims: *"Am I talking to God, or Man! Is it a real Man, or an Angel!"* (*RC*, 254). The captain becomes the first informed reader of Crusoe's story (*RC*, 258). By telling his story, Crusoe makes clear the manifestly providential nature of his intervention in the captain's plight. He has been sent by God, and he acts in harmony with the divine plan.

As a part of his story, Crusoe displays his entire microcosmic civilization to the captain and his two companions. They are properly amazed at his ingenuity (*RC*, 258). Crusoe's entire system of survival is evidence of his success at interpreting his experiences and working in conjunction with the demands of providence and the guidance of reason. The captain has not reached Crusoe's level of enlightenment and is not as skilled at imagining the possible alternatives to his situation. When he seems to fall into a state of despair — a sinful lack of trust with which Crusoe is all too familiar — Crusoe corrects his misapprehension by retelling his story:

> I smil'd at him, and told him, that Men in our Circumstances were past the Operation of Fear: That seeing almost every Condition that could be, was better than that which we were suppos'd to be in, we ought to expect that the Consequence, whether Death or Life, would be sure

> to be a Deliverance: I ask'd him, What he thought of the Circumstances of my Life? And, Whether a Deliverance were not worth venturing for? And where, Sir, said I, is your Belief of my being preserv'd here on purpose to save your Life, which elevated you a little while ago? (*RC*, 260)

He reaffirms the providential aspect of his story and draws attention to their spiritual position: because God is looking after them, even death can hold no threat. Crusoe also invokes his law of contraries. He weighs the alternatives to the path they plan to take and for the first time declares that the situation could hardly be worse. Things can only get better. Crusoe's specific application of the lessons taught by their life stories corrects the captain's tendency to misread the immediate situation. Crusoe demonstrates the level of competence he has reached in discerning what God is trying to tell him through the events in his life.

The captain's recognition is the central prerequisite for Crusoe's repatriation. Unlike the pagans and the Spaniard, the captain shares the same religious faith as Crusoe. Their stories complement each other: both display common elements, recognize the role of providence, and use a similar structure or narrative framework. Crusoe's authority in his interactions with the captain is a further indication of his chosen nature. When he gives himself one identity as a servant and another as the governor of the island, it reflects his dual status as the savior and the one being saved. This is a physical salvation for Crusoe and for the crew of the ship, but he also performs a dual role as spiritual instructor/narrator and still imperfect reader of the divine plan.

After he defeats the mutineers, Crusoe tries to teach them to read the events in their lives as elements in a wider story. He tells the men their own stories and shows them how they demonstrate the action of providence:

> I caused the Men to be brought before me, and I told them, I had had a full Account of their villanous Behaviour to the Captain, and how they had run away with the Ship, and were preparing to commit farther Robberies, but that Providence had ensnar'd them in their own Ways, and that they were fallen into the Pit which they had digged for others. (*RC*, 275)

Most important, Crusoe leaves behind his own account. He emphasizes the completeness of this work (*RC*, 277), so it must include episodes that demonstrate his own sinful behavior. The story shows the mutineers that they should imitate him in their activities and particularly in their thinking. If they become receptive readers of his account, Crusoe's successors may learn how to imitate his success. Affective reading is the necessary precursor to the establishment of a successful society.

Robinson Crusoe is able to return to society because he completely masters himself and his surroundings. He learns to align his actions with the divine plan. An audience that becomes progressively more sophisticated and civilized from Crusoe's perspective acknowledges his authority. Crusoe's acceptance occurs on several parallel levels: his audience accepts his authority in naming, directing, organizing, and governing all aspects of island life. As sympathetic and subservient listeners, they acknowledge the primacy of his past experience. As helpless individuals, they recognize his practical success at surviving and his mechanical accomplishments. As citizens under the common governance of divine providence, they understand God's role in preserving Crusoe, and Crusoe's role in their own lives, as part of a more comprehensive plan. They recognize that Crusoe shows a high degree of spiritual enlightenment, as demonstrated by his ability to discern God's aims.

All of these levels of acceptance depend upon Crusoe's ability to tell his story and show the empirical evidence of his accomplishments. He must share with others the comprehensive organizational system that he has developed for himself in the course of his sojourn on the island. Wandering is only sinful as long as it proceeds from Crusoe's ignorance. Once he has achieved an awareness of his own position in the world and is able to negotiate his path through society on this basis, Crusoe is free to resume his travels.

While Crusoe's story includes episodes that occur outside the island, the desert island part of the text is the aspect that subsequent authors reworked and imitated. As Gisander mentions in his preface to the *Wunderliche Fata*, by 1731 a host of novels had already been written that mimicked *Crusoe* in the hope of imitating the book's success. What is it about *Robinson Crusoe* that cries out for imitation? And why has the desert island motif had such a pervasive and sustained influence on Western culture? Perhaps the best way to answer these questions is to examine some representative readers of the text, summarize their reactions, and discuss what it is about *Robinson Crusoe* that makes it provoke the reactions it does.

The responses of Will Atkins in the sequel to *Crusoe* and of Gabriel Betteredge in Wilkie Collins's novel *The Moonstone* (1868) reflect the effects Crusoe implies his story should have on its readers. After Crusoe leaves, his story forms the basis of the new civilization on the island. In the sequel to

Crusoe, which describes his return to the island, Will Atkins illustrates the importance of imitating the spiritual aspect of the narrative, as well as its practical recommendations, in order to structure the society successfully. Like the unenlightened Crusoe, Will Atkins uses offensive language (*RC,* 268). He has rebelled against the captain, who is a father figure (*RC,* 270), and against his real father.[10] Atkins's transformation from reprobate and quarrelsome rebel into an innovative convert and family man occurs as a result of his imitation of Crusoe's model. His talent for wickerwork designs reflects his ingenuity (*FA,* 3:10). This successful practical application of the principle of rational reflection foreshadows Atkins's eventual religious conversion, which retraces Crusoe's path from natural deduction, through conviction of sin, to the revelation of Christ's forgiveness. Crusoe explicitly compares Atkins's experiences with Crusoe's own conversion, and Atkins's conversations with his wife echo the earlier conversations between Crusoe and Friday (*FA,* 3:44).

As in the other texts, one of the central premises of *Robinson Crusoe* is that reading and interpretation leads to the generation of a story that imitates its source in structure and content. By redeeming himself and telling his story, Crusoe gives others the tools to follow his example. Defoe attributes a high degree of power and authority to Crusoe and to his story. When Will Atkins imitates Crusoe so explicitly, it strengthens the impression that Crusoe's story has the power to transforms its readers' moral, spiritual, and even physical lives. The story Defoe relates is one that aspires to be universal despite its wealth of realistic detail and the apparent uniqueness of Crusoe's situation.

Wilkie Collins's novel *The Moonstone* describes Crusoe's narrative as a second Scripture. Gabriel Betteredge uses *Robinson Crusoe* for guidance in the same way other readers might use a Bible.[11] His reading reflects Crusoe's almost divine role at the end of the story. It also reflects the way that this text — like *Simplicissimus,* as depicted in *Springinsfeld* — tends to usurp some of the functions of Scripture by repeatedly emphasizing its own authority and the affective relationship between the text and its readers.

Betteredge begins his story with a quotation from *Robinson Crusoe.* Later he describes the quotation as a prophecy that warned him about subsequent events.[12] He also discusses at length how he reads *Robinson Crusoe:*

> You are not to take it, if you please, as the saying of an ignorant man, when I express my opinion that such a book as *Robinson Crusoe* never was written, and never will be written again. I have tried that book for

years — generally in combination with a pipe of tobacco — and I have
found it my friend in need in all the necessities of this mortal life. When
my spirits are bad — *Robinson Crusoe*. When I want advice — *Robinson
Crusoe*. In past times when my wife plagued me; in present times when
I have had a drop too much — *Robinson Crusoe*. I have worn out six
stout *Robinson Crusoes* with hard work in my service.[13]

Gabriel Betteredge's way of reading *Robinson Crusoe* is simply a logical exaggeration of what Crusoe and the editor recommend.

The editorial voice in the preface to *Robinson Crusoe* explicitly states that the text provides religious instruction and moral guidance. The story is intended as a model to show readers how to read their own circumstances and how to understand the way providence intervenes in their own lives:

> *The Story is told with Modesty, with Seriousness, and with a religious Application of Events to the Uses to which wise Men always apply them* (viz.) *to the Instruction of others by this Example, and to justify and honour the Wisdom of Providence in all the Variety of our Circumstances, let them happen how they will.* (*RC*, 1)

Betteredge's reaction to the text supports readings of *Crusoe* that focus on the way it uses the structure and language of spiritual autobiography. This text can be read like the Bible because it tries to imitate the latter in terms of function and content. Crusoe himself draws attention to parallels with the story of the prodigal son and the wanderings of the children of Israel in the wilderness, while the sea captain compares him with Jonah at the beginning of the story. More important, Crusoe acts as the hand of God at the end of the island episode. He appears as the miraculous savior of the English captain, who initially perceives him as a messenger from God (*RC*, 254). The episode shows why Betteredge can read — or misread — the text the way he does. Crusoe's narrative becomes a second Scripture because God's action is as visible to Crusoe in his own story as it is in any of the events of the Bible.

The editor also uses the didactic value of *Robinson Crusoe* to justify the possible fictional nature of the work:

> *The Editor believes the thing to be a just History of Fact; neither is there any Appearance of Fiction in it: And however thinks, because all such things are dispatch'd, that the Improvement of it, as well to the Diversion, as to the Instruction of the Reader, will be the same; and as such, he thinks, without farther Compliment to the World, he does them a great Service in the Publication.* (*RC*, 1)

Defoe's text returns to the *prodesse et delectare* justification for fiction that appeared in Grimmelshausen's work. Even if the story is not true, the lessons that it teaches still have a value in terms of the moral and spiritual instruction they provide.

The main difficulty with this argument is that this work of fiction tries to demonstrate how God intervenes in the real world. Despite its wealth of empirical detail, the events in *Robinson Crusoe* did not actually occur and thus can only show how divine providence *might* operate. The author of the work has actually made up the coincidences that demonstrate to Crusoe that providence is directly intervening in his life. I would like to think that Collins recognized this paradox and that it motivated his references to Defoe's text. (It is infinitely appropriate that Defoe's fictional work is capable of providing constructive and even prophetic advice to a fictional character in Collins's fictional work.) The didactic value of the work in illustrating the effect of divine providence on an individual life collapses when the text is read by a real reader in the real world, but it remains safe and free of tension within this fictional context.

Defoe may have intended readers to read his work in the way Gabriel Betteredge does, namely, as a second Scripture, but his imitators find its compelling escapist content a stronger reason to reproduce the story than its value as a religious instruction manual. The satisfaction *Robinson Crusoe* offers is a sophisticated version of the same satisfaction offered by do-it-yourself manuals and gardening books. Defoe includes a wealth of specific details concerning Crusoe's improvements and his progressive domestication and appropriation of the wilderness. Participating in this activity — even if only as a reader of the text — is immensely satisfying. Crusoe is able to directly realize the ideas in his head by inscribing them on the landscape. Readers are not so much interested in the final product of this civilizing activity as in the work itself.

The important difference between Crusoe's experiences and any of his readers' real-life attempts to transform their surroundings is that there is no one — and nothing except, perhaps, his own weaknesses — to stand in the way of Crusoe's activity. He exists in a completely unmediated relationship to his environment. Because he builds his civilization from scratch, it is totally and completely a monument to the strength of his will, the power of his ingenuity and imagination, and his ability of use reason and think sequentially.

Crusoe implies that his readers should respond to this aspect of the text when he leaves his life story behind for the English sailors. Because they are English, he believes they are naturally inclined to be ingenious in a way that the natives and the Spaniards are not. Reading his story will demonstrate to them every particular concerning how they can learn to survive (*RC*, 277). Crusoe has mastered many arts, but he has not mastered all of them. The important lesson of his text is the guidance it gives concerning *how* the sailors must learn to think in order to survive on the island. They must begin to think in a way that is both rational and imaginative, for only then will they be able to master any technical art. They have the chance to transform their surroundings into a pure reflection of their own rational nature and unmediated ingenuity.

Robinson Crusoe does not embrace earthly life and sinful corruption — it still acknowledges that the world is corrupt and rejects the human tendency toward sinfulness — but it is a much more optimistic work than the others discussed in this book. The individual has the power to transform the world around him without needing any special abilities. If the hidden principle that structures all creation is reason, then any rational individual can come to terms with the world and learn to control his surroundings. In this respect Crusoe is more of an Everyman figure than even the allegorical characters in Bunyan's *Pilgrim's Progress*. They are chosen individuals, but readers cannot be entirely sure that God has really included them within this elect group.

The governing principle of Defoe's text is more democratic and less intimidating because it allows the individual to be more active. It seems more feasible to imitate *Crusoe* because he is so dependent on himself. The fictional island appears realistic, but the island civilization completely reflects the plans and efforts of the protagonist. Although readers cannot replicate this unrestrained manifestation of the individual will in their real lives, they can read Crusoe's story again and again for the satisfaction of participating in the process vicariously. The illusions of control, organization, power, and authority are comforting. Above all, the illusion that reason is the fundamental principle of creation, with the power to correct its wildness and corruption, comes as a relief following the sense of chaos and despair that pervades the depiction of worldly life in the other texts. God might not oblige by letting every reader into the Celestial City, but according to *Crusoe* anyone should be able to figure out how to build a hut in the wilderness.

The way Titty in Arthur Ransome's *Swallows and Amazons* (1930) imitates the text[14] reveals the importance of the way the work encourages readers to follow Crusoe's example while remaining a fictional, escapist work. The book strongly encourages imitation, but it is impossible for real readers to reproduce what is, after all, an idealized, fictional situation. As Titty's experiences reveal, the best way to imitate this fictional text is to reread or rewrite the same story.

When the girl goes camping on an island with her brothers and sister, complete isolation is what she really longs for. It will allow her to develop the same sense of mastering her surroundings that Crusoe displays in his story. Ransome uses this material rather cleverly. Titty soon tires of the isolation. On her island, it is impossible to achieve the total dominance of her surroundings that Crusoe achieves on his. The arrangements for her solitary sojourn become meaningless when there is nobody else around to appreciate them. The log she tries to write is like Crusoe's log at the beginning of *Robinson Crusoe;* it lacks purpose, organization, and any sense of progressing toward a goal.[15] Although *Crusoe* is one of her favorite books, there is no use in attempting to imitate her hero. She ends up escaping her loneliness in a more satisfactory way by rereading the book instead.

The fictional nature of this satisfying world is its great strength, but it is also its only weakness. The specific, realistic details in the text create the impression that the island is a viable, comprehensive alternative to the real world. The last thing that readers want to experience is the end of Crusoe's compelling, meticulous development of his surroundings. As Titty concludes:

> But who would wave a flag to be rescued if they had a desert island of their own? That was the thing that spoilt *Robinson Crusoe*. In the end he came home. There never ought to be an end.[16]

The sense of goal-oriented development that structures *Crusoe* demands an ending to the story, but the realistic detail and isolation of the protagonist also strengthen its readers' vicarious participation in the text. Readers like Titty therefore seek the sense of continuity and inclusion that the real ending of the book fails to provide. In order to satisfy readers, Crusoe's work on the island would have to continue, but this is impossible. If the text is designed to illustrate the care of divine providence, Defoe cannot leave Crusoe on the island to face and overcome new hardships in interesting ways. He must return him to England, to his father's station in life, just as the Bible ends with a return to God. Because Defoe's depiction of the island is so convincing, however, he leaves his readers in much the same situation as Bunyan's readers at the end of part 1 of *The Pilgrim's Progress,* who can only pick up the book again and reread the story. Even Crusoe ends his account by revisiting the island (*RC,* 305–6); he wants to know how the story of the island settlement continues.

Authors continue to write books that employ the *Crusoe* situation because Defoe's work stresses the value — and, through its realistic detail, the feasibility — of imitating his model. The story continues in so many other works because Crusoe teaches his readers that any individual can learn to think rationally and mimic his achievements. Readers become Robinsonade addicts because their vicarious participation in the protagonists' civilizing activity disappears when the main characters leave the island. The only satisfactory response to such an ending is to reread the same book or find another book that tells the same story.

Robinson Crusoe's fictional nature may undermine its claimed didactic authority, but the strength of the illusion that the story creates means that the text transforms its readers in a different way. The story of Robinson Crusoe is a great work of escapist fiction. Readers might not *really* want to land on a desert island, but they love to read about what might happen if they did.

Notes

[1] Daniel Defoe, *The Life and Strange Surprizing Adventures of Robinson Crusoe of York, Mariner,* ed. J. Donald Crowley (Oxford: Oxford UP, 1998), 78–79. Subsequent references to this work are cited in the text using the abbreviation *RC* and page number.

[2] See Paul K. Alkon, *Defoe and Fictional Time* (Athens: U of Georgia P, 1979), 188.

[3] See Michael Seidel, *Robinson Crusoe: Island Myths and the Novel* (Boston: Twayne, 1991), 81.

[4] *"How come you here?"* (*RC,* 143).

[5] "my old Hutch," "my own House" (*RC,* 111).

[6] "my Fortification," "my Castle, for so I think I call'd it ever after this" (*RC,* 154). Both examples are pointed out by Robert James Merrett in his *Daniel Defoe's Moral and Rhetorical Ideas* (Victoria, Canada: U of Victoria P, 1980), 87.

[7] For example, the plight of the captain and mates of the ship resembles Crusoe's former plight.

[8] See Erhard Reckwitz, *Die Robinsonade: Themen und Formen einer literarischen Gattung* (Amsterdam: B. P. Grüner, 1976), 223.

[9] See Timothy C. Blackburn, "Friday's Religion: Its Nature and Importance in *Robinson Crusoe*," *Eighteenth-Century Studies* 18 (1984–85): 374.

[10] Daniel Defoe, *The Farther Adventures of Robinson Crusoe Being the Second and Last Part of His Life* (1719; reprint, London: William Clowes, 1974), 3:43–44. Subsequent references to this work are cited in the text using the abbreviation *FA* plus the volume and page number.

[11] See Anthea Trodd, "Notes" to *The Moonstone*, by Wilkie Collins (Oxford: Oxford UP, 1998), 525.

[12] Wilkie Collins, *The Moonstone* (1868; reprint, Oxford: Oxford UP, 1998), 8.

[13] Collins, *The Moonstone*, 9.

[14] Arthur Ransome, *Swallows and Amazons* (London: Jonathan Cape, 1990), 186–93, 203–6.

[15] Ransome, 203.

[16] Ransome, 186.

6: Schnabel's *Wunderliche Fata einiger See-Fahrer* (*Insel Felsenburg*)

TIME HAS NOT BEEN particularly kind to Johann Gottfried Schnabel's *Wunderliche Fata einiger See-Fahrer*. Immensely popular when first published and part of the childhood reading of some of the most important figures of German Romanticism,[1] the first volume barely remains in print. Even the work's most enthusiastic fans — and there are not very many! — admit that it is not a literary masterpiece. Within the present argument, Schnabel's work is important precisely *because* it is neither particularly deep nor extremely original. Schnabel intended his work for popular consumption and he consciously wrote within the already recognizable Robinsonade genre. The *Wunderliche Fata* distills the elements of the Robinsonade for a mass audience, thus revealing a lot about the establishment of the genre. In addition, Schnabel's introduction contains comments that defend the value of fictional, entertaining works. These comments reflect an important transition in the theory of the novel.

The four volumes of the *Wunderliche Fata* appeared in 1731, 1732, 1736, and 1743. The first volume contains one of the eighteenth century's most complete Robinsonade episodes, while subsequent volumes describe the island settlement and relate its inhabitants' life stories. Secondary criticism of the text has tended to focus on the influence of German pietism or Enlightenment rationalism on the author. The general consensus is that life on the utopian island, the Insel Felsenburg, combines an Enlightenment emphasis on order and reason with the overt piety and sentimentality characteristic of German pietism.

The structure of the *Wunderliche Fata* is more complex than that of the other texts. Following an introduction by the fictional editor, Gisander, the story shuttles between the autobiographies of individual characters and the frame narrative, which contains Eberhard Julius's description of how he heard the stories. Although the personalities of individual characters influence the way they tell their stories, almost all of the stories share the same basic premise. Characters endure a period of tortured and aimless wandering through the sinful world. They escape to the island only through the intervention of divine providence. The simple contrast between the wretched condition of characters before reaching the island and their blissful state on the island gives their stories a common structure:

Outside World	*Insel Felsenburg*
• Sin	• Virtue
• Movement	• Rest
• Deception	• Honesty
• Disorder	• Order
• Danger and Destruction	• Stability and Construction
• Passion	• Reason
• Social Alienation	• Social Integration
• Roman Catholics and Calvinists	• Pious Lutherans and (occasionally) Anglicans
• Bad	• Good

The *Wunderliche Fata* is less clearly didactic than the other works under discussion, but it is also less morally ambiguous. A straightforward moral scheme operates on the island: God rewards virtue and punishes evil. This system simply does not function in the outside world. Non-Felsenburgers do not have any sense of living directly under divine supervision.

The split between the outside world and the island, on the one hand, and the theoretical perspective from which the novel was written, on the other, share a common link. In the introduction the editor figure, Gisander, makes what appears to be a fairly clear statement concerning the entertaining qualities of what will follow.[2] His tactic throughout the introduction is to disorient the reader. He begins by refusing to justify the text as a utopia intended to criticize a certain system of government, but he does mention the possibility of reading the text according to this interpretation and leaves the final decision up to the reader (*WF,* 1:ii^r). By denying his text any ideological value, Gisander eliminates the possibility of arguing that the text, although fictional, has didactic value as a moral or allegorical work. Gisander then gives voice to some objections to the Robinsonade in a long passage of scathing criticism. In replying to these accusations, he begins by defending the whole idea of reading for entertainment but refuses to state explicitly whether this work is true or fabricated:

> Allein, wo gerathe ich hin? Ich solte *Dir, geneigter Leser,* fast die Gedancken beybringen, als ob gegenwärtige Geschichte auch nichts anders als pur lautere Fictiones wären? Nein! dieses ist meine Meynung durchaus nicht, jedoch soll mich auch durchaus niemand dahin zwingen, einen Eyd über die pur lautere Wahrheit derselben abzulegen. (*WF,* 1:iii^v)

> [However, where am I going with this? Should I suggest the thought that the present story might be nothing other than pure fiction to you, honored reader? No! This is completely not my opinion, but at the same time no one will force me to swear an oath as to its honest truth.]

He gives the reader a fair indication that this text may — just may — have been made up, and that, if so, it was made up solely as a diversion for the reader. Gisander's argument that the entertainment value might just be enough to justify the fictional nature of his book is quite a departure from the rhetoric concerning the truth and moral value of the text that Defoe and Grimmelshausen use to defend their works.

For my present purposes, the most shocking paragraph in Gisander's argument is his comparison between entertaining fiction and the Bible. He moves a step beyond Bunyan's argument that he is imitating the Bible by using allegory and Grimmelshausen's argument that presenting moral lessons in an entertaining manner makes them more palatable:

> Warum soll denn eine geschickte Fiction, als ein Lusus Ingenii, so gar verächtlich und verwerfflich seyn? Wo mir recht ist, halten ja die Herren Theologi selbst davor, daß auch in der Heil. Bibel dergleichen Exempel, ja gantze Bücher, anzutreffen sind. (*WF,* 1:iii^v)

> [Why should a clever fiction, as an exercise of ingenuity, be so completely despicable and reprehensible? If I am not mistaken, the theologians themselves believe that we meet similar examples, even whole books, in the Holy Bible.]

Gisander is not defending his entertaining stories according to the Horatian *prodesse et delectare* idea. Instead, he justifies the existence of clever fictions because they demonstrate the writer's genius. Although Gisander uses the comparison with the Bible to defend his work, unlike Bunyan he does not say that the stories in the Bible are seemingly fictional works that hold deeper meanings. The stories in the Bible are made up, just like other fantastical stories. They reflect their writer's ingenuity — perhaps even inspiration — as do all clever fictions. Schnabel is broaching a subject that was certainly subversive when the text was published in 1731. With this argument about the value of fiction and his description of the Bible as a book like other books, Schnabel is only a step away from the secularized worship of the literary imagination that appears in German Romanticism.

Despite Gisander's words, the *Wunderliche Fata* is not a text that wholly discards religion. Biblical paradigms and explicit signs of religious faith pervade the lives of the Felsenburg inhabitants. This is, however, a text that uses Scripture only in order to re-create it in the fictional context of the island civilization. Religious belief plays a very small role in the lives of the characters in their existence beyond the island. The corrupt world is a satirical representation of Schnabel's readers' real world, while the regenerate world is a complete fictional construct. The text is an escapist work. Readers encounter the hideous corruption of a fairly realistic world alongside the text's many protagonists. The journey finally takes them to the island, a place of escape. The basis of the utopia is Schnabel's vision of how civilization would be organized *if* the stories related in the Bible were true and *if* God really did intervene in human affairs.

Bunyan displays a sincere belief in the power of the Bible as a transforming text, one his characters may enter and dwell in. Schnabel uses it as the basis for his fictional society. He does indicate to the reader that it may actually be possible to visit the island, but he is primarily using the scriptural paradigms as a vehicle for entertainment, a critical contrast to European society, and a way of creating a pleasing end point for the individual autobiographies. Reading is not a way of transforming the physical here and now, but through reading it is possible to enter an imaginary landscape that can, to some extent, supplant the reader's unpleasant surroundings. It would be hopeless to try to apply the moral norms and spiritual teachings of Scripture to the European world, but the pleasure of reading a book can provide an escape from its endless corruption. Reason may not be the governing principle of life in the outside world, but imagining an island where it does govern existence is a good way of ignoring this fact.

For Schnabel storytelling possesses a fundamental value in and of itself; the Bible is a story among other stories, but it is a good story and a powerful one. Writers, readers, and storytellers create alternate worlds by telling new stories and by reworking and connecting their narratives to old stories. The world Schnabel creates is very complete and quite convincing because of the sheer weight of narration. The *Wunderliche Fata* includes so many stories, is so long, and describes the island and the European world from so many different viewpoints that it seems to take on a reality of its own. It is difficult to disbelieve in a world that appears three-dimensional, and the reactions of readers to the island civilization reflect this.[3]

Events in Schnabel's text are fictional, but they are literal, not allegorical imitations of events in the Bible. This is an important distinction, because discarding allegory creates a very different relationship between the novel and its source text. Bunyan offers his readers an allegorical vision of the earthly paradise. Defoe shows how it might literally be possible to live in a state that is *like* living in an earthly paradise. Schnabel creates what is literally an earthly paradise, a realm whose inhabitants live under God's direct rule in a prelapsarian state.

Like characters in the other texts, individual characters in the *Wunderliche Fata* use biblical paradigms to structure their experiences. Captain Wolffgang, who saves the elect from the corrupt world in his ship, becomes a Noah figure.[4] Eberhard's father compares himself to Job (*WF*, 3:17); the structure of his account mirrors that of Job's story. While he frequently uses biblical references, Schnabel treats his source text in a way that would have been unthinkable to Bunyan or even Defoe. When Albertus and Concordia marry each other, they recite passages from the Book of Tobias, but they alter them in a significant way. They *replace* the names of biblical figures in the passages with their own names and *change* and *expand* the text to make it more applicable to their own situation.[5] By taking liberties with the text of the Bible, they demonstrate that it is not quite universally applicable. They cannot speak through Scripture in the same way that Crusoe or Christian could, and they no longer treat it as a self-interpreting text with its own autonomous authority. Crusoe and Christian must learn how their experiences conform to the authoritative text of the Bible, but Albertus and Concordia can make the Bible conform to their experiences.

Subsequent events demonstrate how Schnabel exaggerates Bunyan's tendency to describe individual experience by speaking through Scripture. Albertus and Concordia imitate Tobias's three nights of chastity before consummating their marriage. They do more than merely imitate a good moral model; they completely reenact the scriptural text, replacing the original letter of Scripture with a living example. Albertus and Concordia hope that this reenactment will result in divine favor (*WF*, 1:268). The biblical text has a certain authority. By reenacting the biblical story, they demonstrate that they are similar to its characters. Because they are doing the same things, they expect to stand in the same relationship to God and to receive the same rewards. The experience of the fictional individual replaces the scriptural figure.

This process of replacing biblical events with fictional events occurs throughout the *Wunderliche Fata,* most centrally when Albertus and Concordia identify themselves as a second Adam and Eve living in the Garden of Eden. When Eberhard lands on the island and hears the stories of the first and second generation of settlers, it is clear that both the native Felsenburgers and the immigrant Europeans feel that they are part of what is literally an elect nation chosen by God for peace and happiness on earth (*WF,* 1:442). The biblical quotations chosen during important events describe the island's history as that of a chosen people. For example, Ps. 107:9 appears as the sermon text during a church service celebrating Eberhard's return to Felsenburg (*WF,* 3:56–57). The quotation mirrors the structure and content of the individual life stories by describing how a chosen individual moves from a state of fear and suffering toward succor and salvation. In the first volume the minister, Magister Schmeltzer, describes the island society as the spiritual daughter of Zion (*WF,* 1:466, Isa. 62:11). When Albertus lies dying, Magister Schmeltzer reads him Jacob's blessing, predictions, and recommendations for his descendants, who form the twelve tribes of Israel (*WF,* 3:237). The Altvater follows Jacob's example and leaves instructions concerning government and possible dangers to his sons. In the fourth volume, during the service to pray for salvation from the earthquake, Schmeltzer reads from Isa. 6:8–13, ending with a verse that identifies the civilization as a holy seed (*WF,* 4:26).

Biblical descriptions of the people of Israel are also the source for the tribal political organization of the island. Albertus Julius II describes himself as a prophet in the final volume (*WF,* 4:17). His position as a visionary leader of a tribal society harks back to Old Testament histories. Ties of blood and marriage bind the island society, and a characteristically Old Testament understanding of the relationship with God governs it. Within the confines of the island, divine law — in this case, the joint rule of the natural order of reason and the revealed order of the Ten Commandments — is paramount. Examples of divine wrath and destruction, like the Flood and Sodom and Gomorrah, warn the Felsenburg inhabitants of the dangers of sin and disobedience. Don Cyrillo de Valaro fears God's wrath due to the sinful sexual exploits of his companions. The earthquake in the fourth volume warns the Felsenburg inhabitants against complacency. The recognition of human impotence counteracts the danger of arrogance in the nation's image of itself as an elect nation. The Felsenburg God is a jealous deity, and the island's inhabitants are completely dependent on divine mercy for their existence and sustenance.

Most of the biblical quotations and examples in the *Wunderliche Fata* come from the Old Testament. Among the many church services and religious festivals occurring on the island, only once is a reading taken from the New Testament, from one of the epistles to the Corinthians. All other cited readings are Psalms and excerpts from Old Testament books, particularly the prophetic Book of Isaiah. Excluding very occasional mentions in the titles of Lutheran hymns, the Felsenburg vocal-music compositions mention Jesus only once (*WF*, 4:36). The sense that this society occupies a privileged position in the hands of the infinitely just God of the Old Testament appears in the novel both implicitly (in the actions and experiences of the islanders) and explicitly (in sermons, songs, and comments). Like the Old Testament God, however, this is a localized deity. The logic that the pious are rewarded and the evil punished appears valid only on the island, which functions as a sort of waiting room for heaven. In the outside world chaos and fortune reign; and virtue has no connection with happiness.

Characters in the works discussed in previous chapters understand their stories by using the Bible to describe their experiences. They arrive at an awareness of the comprehensive nature of the story that the Bible tells. The story is not just limited to the book but extends into the future, as the story of God's entire creation and the individual humans who participate in it. The common structure of these specific life stories reflects the omnipresence of this divine narrative. Creation is in a process of returning to God, but humans can only understand this macrocosmic movement on a microcosmic level. The return to a state of acting in unity and harmony with God is personally significant, but it also demonstrates that the story told in the Bible affects every time period and every level of existence.

Schnabel uses the Bible in quite a different way. His text virtually replaces the New Testament as an entertaining, fictional sequel to the Old Testament. Bunyan condemns himself for thinking he has to be descended from Abraham to be chosen by God, but the members of the Felsenburg tribe are literally Israelites, a chosen people who have reached the Promised Land. Schnabel is not attempting to show his readers how to live within a living text; rather, he is giving them a popular sequel to the Old Testament.

From the perspective of the evolution of the novel, the move toward entertaining, escapist fiction in Schnabel's work already appears implicitly within the works examined in previous chapters. The authors of *The Pilgrim's Progress, Simplicissimus,* and *Robinson Crusoe* emphasize the instructive value of their works because they are conscious that they are writing books that do not really fit into preestablished categories. They bolster this defense by making comparisons between their texts and the Bible in order to give their works some of the latter's authority. They are careful to show their readers that there is a difference between the way good and bad people use language; their narrators claim to use good language. They repeatedly depict the positive value of reading and telling stories within their works to strengthen their completeness and authority and to provide their real readers with positive models for the reception of the text. In short, they use the same techniques that Schnabel uses for the same reasons.

Schnabel's novel may not be as sophisticated as the other works under discussion, but its relative crudity shows how he defends his fiction more clearly. The difference between the way language operates on the island and in the outside world reflects the same division between reprobate and redeemed language that appears in the other works. In the early criticism of the *Wunderliche Fata* Fritz Brüggeman describes the island as an "Insel der Redlichen," where honest discourse contrasts with the lies and intrigue of the outside world.[6] F. J. Lamport criticizes this generalization by pointing out that when they communicate with the outside world the inhabitants of Felsenburg are just as likely to lie as the novel's worldly characters.[7] The split between the two realms is so complete that the code that normally governs the inhabitants of the island simply does not apply when they are interacting with people from the outside world.

As the numerous life stories attest, it is seldom safe for characters residing outside the island to reveal their identities or past experiences. Many of the individual life histories involve episodes of disguise and deception. Abductors sail off with Judith van Manders after inviting her on a harbor cruise. Schimmer disguises himself as a student. David Rawkin's parents disguise themselves to hide from their enemies. Albertus and Concordia disguise themselves to assist van Leuven's plot to run off with Concordia. Lemelie's sister disguises herself as his wife. Outside the island events occur arbitrarily and God seldom punishes sinfulness, so it is just as impossible to look for meaning within personal experience as it is to trust the words of fellow humans.

In contrast, the inhabitants of the island use language in a direct, honest, and utilitarian way. As for Bunyan and seventeenth-century Quakers this includes a repudiation of language that is gratuitously ornamented or artificial. Perhaps the best example occurs when Concordia rebukes Albertus for his flowery love speech (*WF,* 1:264). She explicitly rejects upper-class, polite language in favor of the bourgeois directness that characterizes communication on the island. Beyond its hyperbolic tone, Albertus's speech is flawed because it is too indirect. He says he is honored that Concordia's beautiful hands have troubled themselves to write a letter to him. He claims that it is impossible for words to express her worth and then contradicts himself by using words to try to describe her many attributes (*WF,* 1:264). Through his convoluted descriptions, he denies Concordia direct responsibility for her words. When he claims that language cannot communicate his meaning, he undermines his own integrity by trivializing the truth he tries to convey. According to Concordia, Albertus's virtuous conduct is sufficient proof of his worth. Their situation requires mutual trust and honesty. They must only use language in ways that make the connection between words and their meanings clear; false ornamentation and hypocrisy should be avoided. Within the island society, yes must mean yes, and no must mean no.[8]

The direct, honest communication among Felsenburg's inhabitants mirrors their direct communication with God. Prayers from the Felsenburgers are often efficacious irrespective of whether they are actually on the island or traveling outside it. In contrast, the prayers of travelers from outside are most often ineffective until they reach the island, as is shown in the woeful life story of Virgilia van Cattmer.

In the process of entering the island, characters become able to recognize the workings of divine providence in preserving them from misfortune and destruction. Various signs that the island civilization fulfills some greater divine purpose pervade the island's history. Dreams, ghostly visitations, astrological predictions, and simple hunches play a role in the society's inception and development. Numerous supernatural messages and prophecies hint at the existence of a divine master plan for the island, a destiny greater and more comprehensive than the individual fates described in the personal life stories. The inhabitants of Felsenburg are extremely conscious that the patterns in their individual stories, in the history of the entire settlement, and in their surroundings are significant. They celebrate anniversaries with exemplary rigor and devotion, and they interpret unusual natural and supernatural phenomena in light of their relation to providence and the destiny of the island.

Unlike the world that surrounds it, Insel Felsenburg is a closed and holistic realm. It is an area in which events almost always occur for a reason. With the exception of some of the sensational episodes in the later volumes, new immigrants and fresh discoveries always contribute in some necessary fashion to the perfection of the whole civilization. The inhabitants of the island live together in harmony; their individual stories demonstrate how their particular skills and experience contribute to the development of the island civilization. The tradesmen's stories in the second volume reveal how they learned the trades that contribute to the island's infrastructure. Don Cyrillo de Valaro leaves behind a handy cave and some seeds; more important, he leaves behind his autobiography and other writings to show Albertus and Concordia how to use the island's resources.

The landscape of the island is also full of physical memorials that record the role individual lives have played within the island's comprehensive history. In the cemetery short versions of the life stories decorate the gravestones. When Albertus finally dies in the third volume, his ornate gravestone contains a record of his own life story and the history of the entire society. Memorials of other pertinent occurrences, such as van Leuven's murder and the construction of the church, contribute to the heavily texted topography of the island. Each section of the island is named after its local patriarch, and the focus of the whole is the Alberts-Burg, just as Albertus's story is the dominant narrative in the island's history. Each settler adds some new and necessary element to the infrastructure of the island; the names and memorials show how their individual experiences, as related in the life stories, contribute to the island's destiny.

Because there are such differences between the way communication works on and off the island, entering the island changes the way individual characters view the world around them. The prerequisite to entry and successful settlement on the island is a conversion experience, during which characters completely despair and then resign their wills to the guidance of divine providence. Because the individual narratives are shorter, less psychological, and more anecdotal than those that appear in the texts discussed in previous chapters, they contain less detail concerning the mental aspects of the conversion experience. The focus on plot does emphasize the common elements and conventions of each narrative in much the same way as collections of spiritual biographies or autobiographies tend to stress the common elements of the conversion experience.[9]

For individual characters the conversion experience occurs as a result of recognizing their helplessness and sinfulness and relinquishing their will to God. Each character who enters the island provides a narrative of this movement from ignorance to recognition as a prerequisite for acceptance into the community. The pattern of the conversion narrative is roughly the following:

1. Sinful experience.
2. Danger and crisis.
3. Fear of death and recognition of helplessness.
4. Relinquishing of the individual fate to divine guidance.

This structure appears in the majority of the life stories of the newcomers. The basis of this conversion experience is a recognition of moral extremes and negative possibilities similar to Crusoe's law of opposites. It is only possible to understand the highest good after experiencing the greatest evil. For the characters who relate their stories in the first volume, and for those who arrive, following shipwreck and disaster, in the third and fourth volumes, the experience of despair occurs as a part of the Robinsonade situation. A disaster, usually a storm, leads characters to the island. The sea represents doubt, uncertainty, and the chaotic displacement that characterizes life in the outside world. The island provides rest, but it also represents the sense of certainty and reassurance that individuals receive when they suddenly recognize that God is looking after them.

Having experienced the extreme evils of physical peril and psychological despair, Captain Wolffgang, Virgilia van Cattmer, Amias and Robert Hülter, and Judith van Manders and her companions see the island as the essence of all that is good. Captain Wolffgang and Amias and Robert Hülter mistake the Felsenburgers for angels and the island for heaven (*WF*, 1:292–93). These naturally virtuous characters are thankful for God's intervention, and this prepares them to live under his governance and supervision. Experiencing and overcoming emotional extremes enables the newcomers to understand the natural reason, moderation, and divine benevolence that are the sources of the Felsenburg state and consciously to reject the unbridled and bestial passions that are its enemy.

Although it follows a similar pattern, the route to the earthly paradise, occurs in a slightly different fashion within the narratives of the tradesmen who relate their life stories in the second volume of the *Wunderliche Fata*. Like Eberhard Julius, the men have all intentionally set out for the island. Their arrival does not coincide with a moment of extreme danger, fear, or despair. Instead, the moments of despair and conversion tend to occur earlier in their lives. The characters develop a sense of alienation and disgust with their sinful surroundings. They therefore embrace the opportunity to escape. Even Eberhard Julius only receives an invitation to the island after he has relinquished his will to God following his father's bankruptcy and his own collapse into a sea of confused and chaotic thoughts (*WF,* 1:7).

The narratives of Eberhard's traveling companions follow the pattern set by his own narrative. With the exception of Captain Wolffgang, the characters in the first volume tend to appear as victims of sin, naturally virtuous rather than naturally sinful. The European tradesmen in the second volume, however, relate their stories as moral exempla or cautionary tales. Müller Krätzer, in particular, relates his story as an explicit conversion narrative. He enumerates the violent deeds of his past and recounts the story of his sickness, fear, and progressive religious awakening in terms reminiscent of Bunyan's *Grace Abounding* (*WF,* 2:394–95).

Like Bunyan's scriptural voices, Krätzer's visions appear to him from outside himself. In his sickness he becomes the passive reader of his own experience. His vision of hell causes him to judge the moral value of his actions. Krätzer's recognition that his nature is inherently sinful is the necessary precursor to his conversion as well as that of all the characters in these texts. He wins his subsequent battle against despair by reading religious texts, among them Johann Arndt's *Paradies-Gärtlein* (Garden of Paradise, 1612) and Mayer's *Verlohrnes und wieder gefundenes Kind GOttes* (The Child of God, Lost and Found, 1685). The books help him overcome his doubts by providing advice and examples upon which to model his future behavior (*WF,* 2:396).

These characters are not particularly evil — especially in comparison with truly reprobate characters like Lemelie — but in their stories they become victims of circumstance because they cannot control their emotions. Mathematicus Litzberg's reserved bearing contrasts with his previously feverish and passionate nature. Eberhard comments on Chirurgus Kramer's dry manner of relating his story (*WF,* 2, 236), but the surgeon admits that he possessed a wild and fiery temperament in his earlier days (177). Plager, too, contrasts his former lack of control over his emotions with the moderation he displays on the island (317). Their stories indicate that they have overcome the subjection to original sin visible in their unreasonable passions by learning to think reasonably and act in the rational, controlled manner that is more pleasing to God.

Each of the narrators in the second volume end their stories by confirming that they are part of the island community. Chirurgus Kramer's statement is typical. After being tossed on the waves of misfortune, he has found an earthly paradise. He describes living in the arms of his loving wife and in the midst of pious people and true friends as a foretaste of the joys of heaven (*WF*, 2:235). As an inhabitant of the island, he lives under the direct care of God. Through his marriage he has achieved social integration. He has moved from a state of instability to safety and rootedness, encapsulated in the wave and harbor metaphor. The metaphor reflects the literal and spiritual path he has taken to reach the island, a place of paradisiacal rest, safety, and pleasure.

The life stories of the individuals who enter the island civilization signify a movement from the sinful world to a state of rest and integration. Through the socially constructive processes of narrating and listening — and by repeating the same narrative structure — storytelling consistently reinforces the basic precepts of the Felsenburg civilization. The common ending of each story, namely, the entry into the earthly paradise, affirms the shared structure and similar values of each account. The characters' ability to organize and retell their experiences indicates that they have learned how to use language in a true and rational way.

One of the most interesting things about the frequent use of the conversion narrative structure in the *Wunderliche Fata* is that the island's history follows a similar movement from sin to redemption. It is even possible to provide a specific reading of the initial phase of settlement according to the conversion narrative paradigm. The evil Captain Lemelie is the embodiment of original sin. He accompanies the settlers and is responsible for the destruction of Concordia's first partner, van Leuven, who represents the old Adam. By resisting Lemelie's sexual advances, Concordia is able to reverse the sin of Eve. Lemelie makes a confession and then kills himself; once sin has been acknowledged, recognized, and rejected, it disappears.

Concordia's birth pangs and the birth of the new Concordia follow Lemelie's death. These are the first events in her new relationship with Albertus Julius, the second Adam. The death of the old Adam and the confession and recognition of sin lead to rebirth into a state of redemption. Left alone on the island, Albertus and Concordia regain the constellation of the first family; their marriage creates a redeemed society living in a paradisiacal state. The process of organizing experiences into stories parallels that of developing the island into a paradisiacal civilization. Both activities imitate God's work as the author of creation. They free humans from their subjection to the bestial appetites that accompany original sin.

Schnabel places great emphasis on the socially constructive effects of storytelling. His characters tell stories to amuse and inform each other, but their stories also fill a need beyond mere entertainment. The Felsenburg's inhabitants have a voracious appetite for stories, and they display a delight in narration to the extent that it becomes a life-giving force. The Felsenburgers try to delay the deaths of Lemelie and, later, of another castaway so they can properly recount their horribly thrilling stories. The process of storytelling appears to sustain these characters, for once they have reached a conclusion they die fairly promptly. In one case the need to tell a story even creates life after death. Don Cyrillo de Valaro returns from beyond the grave in order to reveal the location of his story. He later reappears to remind Albertus that he must read it in order to preserve his own life.

The history of the island reflects the importance its inhabitants attach to the process of storytelling and sympathetic listening. When Albertus relates his life story to Concordia for the first time, he notices that she participates vicariously in all of his experiences. She laughs during the funny bits and cries when his story is sad. Once Concordia has finally heard Albertus's complete life story — after more than a year alone with him on the island — her offer of marriage is quick to follow. The account not only fulfills the practical function of assuring her of Albertus's good and trustworthy nature (*WF*, 1:262) but also creates a sense of intimacy. She only allows herself to participate in the intimate relationship between narrator and listener when the period of mourning for her first partner, van Leuven, is over.

Within the individual life stories, including the European portions of the tales, sympathetic listening fulfills a similarly constructive role. Listeners who are willing to hear and understand the whole story of a character's experiences respond positively and benevolently to the plight of the narrator. In the story of Saint Boniface and the ducats, the Roman Catholic bishop gives a true and honest response to a true and honest story (*WF*, 2:338) even though he is a heretic in Tischler Lademann's eyes. The bonds that sympathetic listening creates can temporarily overcome individual characters' isolation. Sympathetic mentors enable them to receive an education or to learn a profession, thereby preparing them to fulfill their professional roles and fit into Felsenburg society when they finally reach the island. Thus, in the story of Mathematicus Litzberg, the sympathetic listener, a Saxon noblewoman, rescues him from the Swedish commander, who is the unsympathetic listener to his true and uncensored tale. These solutions always remain temporary, however. It is not until the characters actually arrive on the island that the social function of their life stories becomes truly effective for the characters who tell them.

Storytelling is the force that sustains the entire society. The life stories in the first volume ensure that the newcomers to the island preserve the memory of the early stages of the island's development. Because they hear accounts of all of the individual experiences that serve as the building blocks of Felsenburg society, the new inhabitants — particularly Eberhard, Wolffgang, and Schmeltzer — develop a connection with the island civilization. When Eberhard sails to the island, Captain Wolffgang's description of how he first entered the island mirrors the journey. The parallel between storytelling and traveling to the island emphasizes the importance of understanding the island's past in order to understand its present. The initial storytelling by Albertus and his sons- and daughters-in-law occurs at the same time as the physical tour Eberhard takes around the island. They return each evening to listen to stories told at the island's central seat of government, the Alberts-Burg. This circular tour confirms that Eberhard has overcome the aimless wandering that marks his life story. Journeying through the landscape reveals the meaning of particular past events to its inhabitants, as well as the significance of the island's topography.

The social and political function of the life stories appears most clearly and systematically in the second volume. Social position rather than chronological considerations determines the order in which the newcomers relate their autobiographies. Herr Magister Schmeltzer, the Lutheran pastor, sets up a paradigmatic structure when he tells his story. He glosses his own tale by adding a moral verse at the end to underline its exemplary value, a feature not present in any of the stories in the earlier volume. Next come the stories of the most educated and authoritative newcomers, Mathematicus Litzberg, Chirurgus Kramer, and Mechanicus Plager. Finally, the tradesmen tell their life stories in order of level of education.

The conclusions of the life stories are always similar. Each character emphasizes the blessed nature of life on the island, expresses his contentment with living piously and quietly, repents of past excesses, describes the stability and personal happiness that is the result his marriage with a native Felsenburg woman, and wishes that he may be of use — particularly in the context of his profession — to his friends on the island and to the island civilization as a whole. All of the narratives perform a similar function by assuring the acceptance of the newcomers by the Felsenburg natives.

Several additional circumstances bolster this impression. In the first volume Captain Wolffgang plays an important role as a mediator between the outside world and the island. He not only brings the newcomers to the island, but his story serves as the model for the life stories that appear later. The individual life stories in the second volume depict Wolffgang as a messenger sent by providence. He bridges the gap between the reprobate world and the earthly paradise and conveys the repentant and displaced sinners to salvation. The first two stories in the second volume appear concurrently with events by means of which Wolffgang seals his own membership in the Felsenburg society, namely, his marriage and the baptism of his first child (*WF*, 2:2–6, 82). These moments are collectively significant for the whole community. The celebrations involve the entire population. They are symbols of the union between the new generation of immigrants and the original Felsenburg inhabitants.

When Litzberg ends the second autobiography following the christening, a delegation of newcomers and Felsenburgers surrounds the group of listeners. They all wish to be married as soon as possible. From among the listeners, Schmeltzer and Litzberg confess that they, too, have found partners. All of the newcomers except Eberhard, who is already connected to the local population by blood, get married at the same time. Following this mass marriage, the stories occur at moments that demonstrate how efficiently and constructively the newly integrated individuals carry out their tasks as part of Felsenburg society. Readers review their accomplishments on the island at the same time they hear the stories of how they got to the island. The characters tell their stories in the districts where they now live and work. Each of the tradesmen has found his place and his calling.

There is a second stage in the storytelling process, namely, the reception of the narratives by the listeners. Eberhard reveals the emotional and sympathetic connection between the storyteller and his audience on the occasions when he appreciatively describes the way the story is told. The listeners to the life stories, led by Albertus Julius in his priestly and patriarchal role, develop a common consensus in interpreting the accounts. They frequently discuss aspects of the story they have heard. In one case Albertus Julius even provides a biblical interpretation of the narrative. Müller Krätzer concludes his account somewhat ashamedly. He is obviously concerned that the confession of his past sins may influence his acceptance in the present. Albertus

Julius reassures him by telling him that his listeners must follow the teachings of the Bible and be grateful for his conversion. According to Albertus, Krätzer's story reveals that he has been a special recipient of divine grace, and these days there are only too few examples of true repentance and reformation. The consensus of his virtuous listeners seals Krätzer's acceptance by the society. His formal acceptance by the head of a country governed according to scriptural law confirms the sincerity of Krätzer's spiritual conversion and moral reformation.

The audience's reactions to the stories are not always completely positive. At the end of Mechanicus Plager's story, the group debates the rights and wrongs of his past conduct. They enumerate his sins and show how his past mistakes have a positive value because they warn others. They criticize Plager for not learning from his father's example. He has failed to recognize the didactic value of bad experiences. Plager's example also underscores the importance of avoiding bad company, particularly those of other confessions. Reprobate characters do not use language in the same honest way or possess the same understanding of divine law as the upright citizens of the island. The narrative process confirms the acceptance of individuals into the society, but it also reinforces social norms through the process of listening, discussion, and mutual consensus.

On the Insel Felsenburg autobiographical narration performs a role very similar to that which it plays in *The Pilgrim's Progress*. In addition to cementing the ties of blood and marriage that structure the society at the time when Eberhard Julius first encounters it, narrative creates a sense of community that transcends time. Through the processes of storytelling and sympathetic listening, the characters in the novel — as well as the readers of the text — come to understand the past history and the values of the island settlement. Like the representatives of the early church, whose stories Christian reads in the House Beautiful, the similarities between the stories of the founders of the Felsenburg society and those of the newcomers emphasize the existence of a continuous community based on a single narrative model and a shared set of norms and referents. Descriptions of the island and the activities of its inhabitants focus on these referents. Eberhard's narrative continually draws attention to significant elements of the Felsenburg topography, man-made memorials to past events, and celebrations of important anniversaries and birthdays. The lives of characters from the past are constantly present, structuring the daily lives of the inhabitants. The fictional text is itself a multilayered narrative, but it is equally true that listening and storytelling structure life on the island.

Schnabel's *Wunderliche Fata,* like Bunyan's *Pilgrim's Progress,* is full of writers and readers, storytellers and listeners. The sheer volume of storytelling activity implicitly tends to include the reader. Following the model of the characters in the novel, readers should form a sympathetic audience, participate vicariously in the reported events, and learn from the moral lessons of the life stories. The sheer breadth and particularity of Schnabel's vision creates this verisimilitude and fosters a sense of inclusion. Several narrators describe the island in thorough detail at different stages in its history. The use of documentary material — maps, genealogical tables, dinner seating plans, sermons, cantatas, organ specifications, letters, and diagrams — combined with Schnabel's tendency to borrow events and anecdotes from nonfiction texts, reinforces the illusion of empirical realism. Certain physical riddles and puzzles that appear on Klein Felsenburg — the urns and the pagan temple — reinforce the sense of continuity in the island's history. Their mysteries are only partially resolved by the end of the fourth volume. This unfinished business strengthens the impression that the island's story extends from its past into the present and the future. At the end of the fourth volume, Gisander's knowing wink and partial explanation of the meaning of the pagan altars humorously signal Schnabel's hidden role as an all-knowing creator. At the same time, however, the remaining mysteries of the text and Gisander's own final submersion into it, in terms of his projected journey to the island, seem to provide it with an autonomous reality beyond its mortal editor.

The sense of inclusion in the text is also the product of the illusion of two-way communication between the island and the European world. Characters constantly move from the world of the actual reader of Schnabel's time to Felsenburg. Eberhard Julius, Captain Wolffgang, and Captain Horn make multiple trips between these two worlds. Gisander, as the European editor of the text, is the first of its readers. Despite his comments in the introduction, he treats the text as an account of an actual society in a real location when making plans to travel to the island. The text creates the overwhelming illusion that its readers could join the Felsenburg society if only they could find a map pointing the way to the island.

Schnabel's work encourages his readers to leave the European world behind. Apart from the moral tags appended to the life stories in the second volume in order to justify their sensationalistic content, the book provides no hope, practical advice, or even explicit criticism that might lead to the positive transformation of the life or the society of the reader. Schnabel's text marks a radical departure from the theoretical perspective of the previous texts. Bunyan wrote *The Pilgrim's Progress* specifically to provide guidance to his readers, to entice them to undertake the same journey toward salvation taken by Christian. Grimmelshausen's *Simplicissimus* claims to use the medium of entertaining stories to educate the reader. *Robinson Crusoe* claims to have been written in order to provide an example to the reader, to demonstrate the workings of divine providence. Schnabel's text, by contrast, is "Curieusen Lesern aber zum vermuthlichen Gemüths-Vergnügen ausgefertiget" (*WF,* title page). It is written for the pleasure and amusement of an audience of curious readers.

Schnabel's *Wunderliche Fata einiger See-Fahrer* has much in common with *Simplicissimus*. The works were both written within the tradition of German anecdotal literature. They both describe a world that is unpleasant and fraught with danger. They both interweave fiction and history by including descriptions of historical occurrences and references to other literary works. In terms of its relationship to the reader, however, Schnabel's text has progressed a stage beyond Grimmelshausen's. It is more unapologetically entertaining, albeit less funny. The satirical aspect of the text is sometimes implied, but it is not explicit. Schnabel substitutes a simple gratification of the reader's escapist desires for Grimmelshausen's attempt at moral instruction. In the *Wunderliche Fata* despair over the presence and influence of God in the real world is total and complete. The only possible hope of seeing things work as they should is leaving the world entirely and traveling to the island, where everything does work properly. The problem is that the island is entirely fictional. Readers can only go there in their imaginations. Whereas Grimmelshausen tries to show people how to cope with the world around them — thereby affirming its value — Schnabel simply shows them how to ignore it.

At the same time, the fictional island is very convincing precisely because the illusion it creates is so complete.[10] The sense of entertainment and satisfaction that readers originally found in the text sustained the popularity of the work for half a century beyond the decade or so it took Schnabel to produce the four volumes. Readers enjoyed — and still occasionally enjoy — the work for the same reason that they might prefer the ending of the second part over the first part of Bunyan's *Pilgrim's Progress*. The fictional society has an autonomous reality of its own. The book ends, but its emphasis on the continual extension of the storytelling process reassures the reader that the story is not really over. Even though there are no words left to read, stories are still being created, told, and listened to. The reader remains a part of the narrative community that the text creates.

The book is escapist, and it is this sense of escape into an alternative world, a self-sustaining world of stories, that is Schnabel's most important contribution to the development of the novel. Storytelling needs no didactic justification. The use of the imagination to generate and appreciate narrative has a value in and of itself. Storytelling may have positive effects, but these are secondary. The value and power of the story is simply that it is a story, a work with a beginning, a middle, and an end. There is satisfaction in the storytelling process. Taking pleasure in stories — whatever their subject, their truth, and their application may be — is a fundamental aspect of human nature. Even if they are pure products of the imagination, stories create their own reality.

Notes

[1] See Volker Meid and Ingeborg Springer-Strand, "Nachwort" to *Insel Felsenburg*, by Johann Gottfried Schnabel (Stuttgart: Reclam, 1979), 594–95, 598–99.

[2] Johann Gottfried Schnabel, *Wunderliche Fata einiger See-Fahrer*, 4 vols. (Frankfurt am Main: Minerva, 1973), 1:ii^r. Subsequent references to this work are cited in the text using the abbreviation *WF* plus the volume and page number.

[3] "Schnabels Beschreibung des Inselparadieses soll sogar manchen jungen Menschen verführt haben, 'auf eine abentheuerliche Weise die glückliche Republik des Altvaters Julius, wo möglich, in der Ferne aufzusuchen.'" J. Chr. L. Haken: *Bibliothek der Robinsone*, vol. 4 (Berlin, 1807); quoted in Meid and Springer-Strand, "Nachwort," 594. (Schnabel's description of the island paradise supposedly seduced some young people "into seeking the happy paradise of Julius, the Altvater, somewhere far away.") An argument about the autonomous reality of the Insel Felsenburg even appears in the twentieth century: in several amusing radio broadcasts Arno Schmidt argues with vigor that the Insel Felsenburg was a spookily prophetic precursor to the actual history and settlement of the island Tristan da Cunha. See Arno Schmidt, "Johann Gottfried Schnabel," *Das Essayistische Werk zur Deutschen Literatur in 4 Bänden. Band 1: Sämtliche Nachtprogramme und Aufsätze* (Zurich: Haffmans, 1988).

[4] See Nicholas Saul, "The Motif of Baptism in Three Eighteenth-Century Novels: Secularization or Sacralization?" *German Life and Letters* 39 (1986): 115.

[5] "Ich aber schlug das 8. Cap. im Buch Tobiä auf, und betete des jungen Tobiä Gebeth vom 7. biß zu ende des 9ten Verses; wiewol ich etliche Worte nach unserm Zustande veränderte, auch so viel zusetzte als mir meines Hertzens heilige Andacht eingab" (*WF*, 1:266–67). (I, however, opened the eighth chapter of the Book of Tobias and prayed the prayer of the young Tobias from the seventh to the end of the ninth verse, and added as much to it as my heart's holy devotion inspired me.)

[6] Fritz Brüggeman, *Utopie und Robinsonade: Untersuchungen zu Schnabels Insel Felsenburg, 1731–1743* (Weimar: Alexander Duncker, 1914), 43.

[7] F. J. Lamport, "Utopia and Robinsonade: Schnabel's *Insel Felsenburg* and Bachstrom's *Land der Inquiraner*," Oxford German Studies 1 (1966): 13.

[8] "Hier ist ja, ja, und nein ist nein. / Hier wird durch falschen Schein / Kein zugesagtes Wort gebrochen" (*WF*, 2:448). (Here yes is yes, and no is no. / Here no promised word is broken / by means of false appearance.)

[9] A typical example is Johann Henrich Reitz's *Historie der Wiedergebohrnen,* vol. 1, pts. 1–3 (1698–1701), ed. Hans-Jürgen Schrader (Tübingen: Niemeyer, 1982).

[10] In *Anton Reiser* Karl Philipp Moritz writes that after reading Schnabel's novel his protagonist wants nothing more than to collect an ever-widening circle of people, plants, animals, and things around himself in imitation of Albertus Julius. Moritz, *Anton Reiser,* ed. Wolfgang Martens (Stuttgart: Reclam, 1972), 34; quoted in Meid and Springer-Strand, "Nachwort," 595.

Conclusion

Throughout *Grace Abounding* and *The Pilgrim's Progress* Bunyan tries to show that the search for salvation is not a straightforward progression. The belief in the effectiveness of good works is one of his greatest temptations. It would be reassuring to be able to climb a ladder toward God, and it would certainly give his autobiography a more systematic structure and a clear sense of development leading to a happy ending.

If achieving salvation were merely a process of satisfying a specific set of moral guidelines or requirements, the authors of the texts discussed in this book would be able to tell their readers exactly how to get to heaven. Instead, these works claim that the gradual effort to achieve virtuous living has no value without the conversion experience that results from God's sudden intervention in the life of the passive individual. This experience of redemption is beyond human understanding. It is therefore impossible to express it to the reader in a way that will allow the latter to participate fully in the experience.

Crusoe, the travelers to Felsenburg, Simplicius, and Christian attempt to understand their experiences by documenting and analyzing them; they seek one set of meanings according to which they can interpret their observations. Tensions and paradoxes accompany their attempts. Language cannot express the inexpressible. If the story ends with a vision of salvation that is transcendent, it leaves behind its reader and, indeed, its author.

All of these authors nevertheless retain their faith in the transforming power of the story. They present storytelling as a divine activity by depicting protagonists who learn to understand and retell their stories as one aspect of the larger story of creation. God is a storyteller — the world is His story — and by imitating God and telling stories, narrators show that they have become godlike. There is more to their powers than simple piety. They actually become agents for the redemption of their surroundings. Like Christ, they are saviors whose stories heal a corrupt world. Like God, these narrators have the power to create a paradise.

Even though these four authors find it unsatisfactory to conclude their stories with a transcendent ending, they try to imitate the Bible in various other ways in order to reassure their readers about the moral value of their texts. One of the most important aspects of the biblical paradigm is its strong teleological impulse; the ending of the biblical story, the return to God, gives meaning to the whole. These authors try to imitate the Bible's simultaneous closure and continuity by providing endings that are not transcendent. The conclusions of these works describe the social communities founded by the storytelling process. They thus provide the reader with a sense of participation and inclusion in the story that continues beyond its ending. They reinforce the sense that the story creates its own autonomous reality. The shift from a transcendent ending to one that depicts a positive social community occurs between the endings of part 1 and part 2 of *The Pilgrim's Progress*, as well as between the endings of *Simplicissimus* and *Springinsfeld*. The shift from the allegorical to the fictional is even more strongly present in *Robinson Crusoe*, reaching its apex in the complete and systematically organized society presented in Schnabel's *Wunderliche Fata*.

The shift from spiritual enlightenment to earthly rootedness parallels the greater attention lavished on the specific details of earthly life. The high degree of verisimilitude and the wealth of specific detail in *Robinson Crusoe* and in the *Wunderliche Fata* reflect the movement away from interpreting the spiritual realm toward observing the empirical world. The realistic detail in these works is a departure from the conventions of previous works of literature, making it imperative for their authors to justify the value of their texts.

The title pages and prefaces to sixteenth-century German books of amusing anecdotes like *Das Lalebuch* (1597) and *Ein kurtzweilig Lesen von Dil Ulenspiegel* (Till Eulenspiegel, 1515) make no attempt to justify their content as having any didactic merit. These works are written to amuse their audience. Their truth is completely irrelevant because their entertaining content justifies itself. Grimmelshausen and Schnabel write within the tradition of the German *Schwankerzählung*, but in both cases criticism forces them to take a defensive position. They protect their texts by using the fiction of the found manuscript. In the introduction to his second volume Schnabel even replies to his critics by using the old argument concerning the didactic value of the stories to justify their often crass content. Defoe uses similar techniques in the preface to *Crusoe*, where he claims that it is an instructive text and that the editor believes the work to be true. Defending himself from criticism after the publication of the book, Defoe even claims that it is actually an allegory. Why do these authors feel impelled to defend their texts when earlier authors of works just as preoccupied with sinfulness and trickery do not? Why do Defoe and Schnabel shy away from admitting that it is possible that their texts are works of fiction?

There are additional questions that need to be asked about these texts. When they are introducing and defending their fictional works, these authors present explicit arguments concerning their books' value to the reader. In addition, all four authors repeatedly include self-reflexive elements in their texts. They show characters developing, telling, reading, and responding to stories. Almost invariably participation in the narrative process, whether by reading or generating a story, has positive results either in terms of the individual's ability to understand his or her surroundings or in creating a sympathetic bond between the isolated individual and other members of society. As I have stated repeatedly, each of the fictional texts depicts a set of exemplary or model readers, characters who, by responding positively to the life stories of other characters, show the real readers how to interpret the text. All of the works discussed are preoccupied — indeed, almost obsessed — with the storytelling process. Important eighteenth-century novels like *Pamela* and *Tristram Shandy* display a similar obsession with how the story is told, but the motif appears only occasionally thereafter, at least until the twentieth century. Why is the storytelling motif so pronounced in these works?

The answer to these questions lies in the transitional status of these fictional texts. They are the result of varying and combining established genres at a time before readers had developed a specific idea about what to expect when they picked up a long fictional narrative. The works of Grimmelshausen and Schnabel combine material from anecdotal literature with the structure of spiritual autobiography. In *The Pilgrim's Progress* Bunyan does something similar, combining spiritual autobiography and the tales of chivalry he read as a child. Grimmelshausen, Defoe, and Schnabel all borrow from the real historical events of their times. Bunyan uses the form of the religious dialogue to structure his characters' conversations. Defoe and Schnabel lean heavily on newspaper accounts and other nonfiction texts for their material.

Bunyan's introduction to *Grace Abounding* is the direct opposite of the prefaces to the German anecdote books — his work is educational, not amusing — but he is similarly confident. He *knows* that his work has a didactic and exemplary value for the congregation of believers that it addresses. Instead of apologizing for having published the work, he assures his reader that it was his *duty* to write it. His tone contrasts sharply with his insecurity in the introduction to *The Pilgrim's Progress,* where he seems reluctant to assert his authority. He claims that the text was written to please himself, not with publication in mind. He depicts the process of writing it as a kind of revelation, but he still tries to preempt criticism of the structure and style of the text by drawing attention to its possible value in instructing the reader.

Because all four authors are writing outside of a clear set of genre guidelines or distinctions, they are acutely conscious of their vulnerability to criticism. The element of the texts about which they seem to anticipate the greatest objection is the most innovative aspect: these texts appear real even though they are made up. Bunyan is concerned that his story is too prosaic, lowly, and crude. Grimmelshausen tells his readers that the specific details and funny incidents he describes in the work mask a set of serious moral lessons. Defoe says that his work is so realistic that it could have happened, adding that the story has a sufficiently useful moral that it does not really matter whether it is empirically true. At the same time as they are busily defending the moral value of their texts, however, these authors are paying progressively more attention to the realistic, social aspects of their stories. They use their fictions to try to convince the reader that storytelling has its own fundamental value, whether the story is true or not.

By the time Schnabel writes the *Wunderliche Fata,* the editor of the text is almost brave enough proudly to defend the genre in which he writes as fictional. His revolutionary attitude toward the Bible — it is just one book among others rather than *the* paradigmatic Book — reflects this new confidence in the value of fiction. It is based on his understanding of the positive value of reading. It does not matter substantially whether his book teaches a significant moral lesson, nor is there any need for his book to lean on another, more authoritative text to justify its existence. A book has its own value because it is a story, and stories divert their readers by creating their own reality.

The tensions in Bunyan's and Grimmelshausen's works explain why *Robinson Crusoe* and the *Wunderliche Fata* move from an emphasis on spiritual and moral enlightenment to one on fictional, earthly fulfillment. Although these texts cannot give salvation to their readers, their realistic emphasis on human psychology and interaction has a constructive and comforting effect on their audience. The worlds they create form a believable and attractive alternative to the world in which their readers live.

By combining realistic fiction with a satisfying religious element and an emphasis on the rule of reason, the novels of Defoe and Schnabel provide a convincing sense of escape. The foundation of their readers' satisfaction is the sense that they participate in a world systematically constructed by means of the storytelling process. The verisimilitude of Crusoe's story underpins a reassuring sense of the world's rational organization. Crusoe's ability to dominate his surroundings by understanding and telling his story reinforces the illusion — on what is already quite a secular level — that the world can be mastered by using logic and language. The complex narrative structure of the *Wunderliche Fata* includes its readers in the fictional community of storytellers and listeners. In order to enter this world, all readers have to do is pick up a book.

The tensions that pervade these texts reflect the difficulties their authors encounter when they try to write books that will bind together a world that seems to be falling apart. If their works cannot fully reinstate the reader's direct communication with God, they are at least able to create alternative worlds in which such a bond does exist. The real world may be a senseless and confusing place, but on Crusoe's island and the Insel Felsenburg yes means yes and no means no. Generating and reading stories has a fundamental value in and of itself. By using their imagination, readers can return to paradise.

Works Cited

Primary Literature

Anon. *Das Lalebuch*. Ed. Stefan Ertz. Stuttgart: Reclam, 1998.

Arnd[t], Johann. *Vier Bücher vom Wahren Christenthum*. Ed. D. Joachim Langen. Halle: Verlag des Wäysenhauses, 1734.

Blumenberg, Hans. *Die Lesbarkeit der Welt*. Frankfurt am Main: Suhrkamp, 1981.

The Book of Common Prayer, 1662. Cambridge: Cambridge UP, 1968.

Browne, Thomas. *Religio Medici (1643)*. Menston, U.K.: Scolar, 1970.

Bunyan, John. *Grace Abounding to the Chief of Sinners*. Ed. Roger Sharrock. Oxford: Clarendon, 1962.

———. *The Pilgrim's Progress from this World to That which is to Come*. Ed. J. B. Wharey and Roger Sharrock. Oxford: Clarendon, 1960.

Collins, Wilkie. *The Moonstone* Ed. Anthea Trodd. Oxford: Oxford UP, 1998.

Defoe, Daniel. *The Farther Adventures of Robinson Crusoe Being the Second and Last Part of His Life*. The Shakespeare Head Edition of the Novels and Selected Writings of Daniel Defoe. Vols. 2 and 3. London: William Clowes, 1974.

———. *The Life and Strange Surprizing Adventures of Robinson Crusoe of York, Mariner*. Ed. J. Donald Crowley. Oxford: Oxford UP, 1998.

Fox, George. *The Journal of George Fox*. Ed. John L. Nickalls. Cambridge: Cambridge UP, 1952.

Grimmelshausen, Hans Jakob Christoph von. *Der Abentheurliche Simplicissimus Teutsch und Continuatio des abentheurlichen Simplicissimi*. Ed. Rolf Tarot. Tübingen: Niemeyer, 1967.

———. *Der seltzame Springinsfeld*. Ed. Franz Günter Sieveke. Tübingen: Niemeyer, 1969.

Ransome, Arthur. *Swallows and Amazons*. London: Jonathan Cape, 1990.

Schnabel, Johann Gottfried. *Wunderliche Fata einiger See-Fahrer*. Vols. 1–4. Frankfurt am Main: Minerva, 1973.

Secondary Literature

Alkon, Paul K. *Defoe and Fictional Time*. Athens: U of Georgia P, 1979.

Almond, Philip C. *Heaven and Hell in Enlightenment England*. Cambridge: Cambridge UP, 1994.

Alpaugh, David J. "Emblem and Interpretation in *The Pilgrim's Progress*." *ELH* 33 (1966): 299–314.

Alt, Johannes. *Grimmelshausen und der Simplicissimus*. Munich: C. H. Beck, 1936.

Baudach, Frank. *Planeten der Unschuld — Kinder der Natur: Die Naturstandsutopie in der deutschen und westeuropäischen Literatur des 17. und 18. Jahrhunderts*. Tübingen: Niemeyer, 1993.

Blackburn, Timothy C. "Friday's Religion: Its Nature and Importance in *Robinson Crusoe*." *Eighteenth-Century Studies* 18 (1984–85): 360–82.

Bloedau, Carl August von. *Grimmelshausens Simplicissimus und seine Vorgänger: Beiträge zur Romantechnik des siebzehnten Jahrhunderts*. Berlin: Mayer & Müller, 1908.

Breuer, Dieter. "Grimmelshausens simplicianische Frömmigkeit: Zum Augustinismus des 17. Jahrhunderts." *Chloe* 2 (1983): 213–52.

Brüggeman, Fritz. *Utopie und Robinsonade: Untersuchungen zu Schnabels Insel Felsenburg, 1731–1743*. Weimar: Alexander Duncker, 1914.

Busch, Walter. "Die Lebensbeichte einer Warenseele: Satirische Aspekte der Schermesser-Allegorie in Grimmelshausens *Continuatio*." *Simpliciana* 9 (1987): 49–63.

Gaede, Friedrich. "Das 'Beschreiben' bei Grimmelshausen," *Simpliciana* 12 (1990): 179–93.

———. *Poetik und Logik: Zu den Grundlagen der literarischen Entwicklung im 17. und 18. Jahrhundert*. Bern: Francke, 1978.

Gebauer, Hans Dieter. *Grimmelshausens Bauerndarstellung: Literarische Sozialkritik und ihr Publikum*. Marburg: Elwert, 1977.

Gerhard, Melitta. "Grimmelshausens 'Simplicissimus' als Entwicklungsroman." In *Der Simplicissimusdichter und sein Werk*, ed. G. Weydt, 133–60. Darmstadt: Wissenschaftliche Buchhandlung, 1969.

Gersch, Hubert. *Geheimpoetik: Die "Continuatio des abentheurlichen Simplicissimi" interpretiert als Grimmelshausens verschlüsselter Kommentar zu seinem Roman*. Tübingen: Niemeyer, 1973.

Geulen, Hans. "'Verwunderungs und Aufhebens werth': Erläuterungen und Bedenken zu Grimmelshausens *Simplicissimus Teutsch*" [special issue: *Grimmelshausen und seine Zeit: Die Vorträge des Münsteraner Symposions zum 300. Todestag des Dichters*, ed. G. Weydt and R. Wimmer]. *Daphnis* 5, nos. 2–4 (1976): 199–215.

———. "Wirklichkeitsbegriff und Realismus in Grimmelshausens *Simplicissimus Teutsch*." *Argenis* 1 (1977): 31–40.

Greaves, Richard L. *John Bunyan*. Appleford, Berkshire, U.K.: Sutton Courtenay, 1969.

Gundolf, Friedrich. "Grimmelshausen und der Simplicissimus." In *Der Simplicissimusdichter und sein Werk*, ed. G. Weydt, 111–32. Darmstadt: Wissenschaftliche Buchhandlung, 1969.

Haller, William. *Foxe's Book of Martyrs and the Elect Nation*. London: Jonathan Cape, 1963.

Hardin, Richard F. "Bunyan, Mr. Ignorance, and the Quakers." *Studies in Philology* 69 (1972): 496–508.

Jöns, Dietrich Walter. *Das "Sinnen-Bild": Studien zur allegorischen Bildlichkeit bei Andreas Gryphius*. Stuttgart: Metzler, 1966.

Kayser, Wolfgang. *Die Wahrheit der Dichter: Wandlung eines Begriffes in der deutschen Literatur*. Hamburg: Rowohlt, 1959.

Keeble, N. H. *The Literary Culture of Nonconformity in Later Seventeenth-Century England*. Avon, U.K.: Leicester UP, 1987.

Lamport, F. J. "Utopia and Robinsonade: Schnabel's *Insel Felsenburg* and Bachstrom's *Land der Inquiraner*." *Oxford German Studies* 1 (1966): 10–30.

Mack, Phyllis. *Visionary Women: Ecstatic Prophecy in Seventeenth-Century England*. Berkeley: U of California P, 1992.

Meid, Volker, and Ingeborg Springer-Strand. "Nachwort" to *Insel Felsenburg*, by Johann Gottfried Schnabel. Stuttgart: Reclam, 1979.

Merrett, Robert James. *Daniel Defoe's Moral and Rhetorical Ideas*. Victoria, Canada: U of Victoria P, 1980.

Owens, W. R. Introduction to *Grace Abounding to the Chief of Sinners*, by John Bunyan. Harmondsworth, U.K.: Penguin, 1987.

Reckwitz, Erhard. *Die Robinsonade: Themen und Formen einer literarischen Gattung.* Amsterdam: B. P. Grüner, 1976.

Reiss, Timothy J. *The Discourse of Modernism.* Ithaca, NY: Cornell UP, 1982.

Reitz, Johann Henrich. *Historie der Wiedergebohrnen.* Vol. 1, Pts. 1–3 (1698–1701). Ed. Hans-Jürgen Schrader. Tübingen: Niemeyer, 1982.

Rivers, Isabel. "Grace, Holiness, and the Pursuit of Happiness: Bunyan and Restoration Latitudinarianism." In *John Bunyan: Conventicle and Parnassus, Tercentenary Essays,* ed. N. H. Keeble, 45–69. Oxford: Clarendon, 1988.

Rohrbach, Günter. *Figur und Charakter: Strukturuntersuchungen an Grimmelshausens Simplicissimus.* Bonn: H. Bouvier, 1959.

Rötzer, Hans Gerd. *Picaro — Landstörtzer — Simplicius: Studien zum niederen Roman in Spanien und Deutschland.* Darmstadt: Wissenschaftliche Buchhandlung, 1972.

Saul, Nicholas. "The Motif of Baptism in Three Eighteenth-Century Novels: Secularization or Sacralization?" *German Life and Letters* 39 (1986): 107–33.

Schmidt, Arno. "Johann Gottfried Schnabel." *Das Essayistische Werk zur deutschen Literatur in 4 Bänden.* Band 1: *Sämtliche Nachtprogramme und Aufsätze.* Zurich: Haffmans, 1988.

Schmitt, Axel. "Intertextuelles Verwirrspiel: Grimmelshausens Simplicianische Schriften im Labyrinth der Sinnkonstitution." *Simpliciana* 15 (1993): 69–87.

Scholte, Jan Hendrik. *Der Simplicissimus und sein Dichter: Gesammelte Aufsätze.* Tübingen: Niemeyer, 1950.

Seidel, Michael. *Robinson Crusoe: Island Myths and the Novel.* Boston: Twayne, 1991.

Sharrock, Roger. Introduction to *The Pilgrim's Progress,* by John Bunyan. Harmondsworth, U.K.: Penguin, 1987.

Smith, Nigel. *Perfection Proclaimed: Language and Literature in English Radical Religion, 1640–1660.* Oxford: Clarendon, 1989.

———, ed. *A Collection of Ranter Writings from the Seventeenth Century.* London: Junction, 1983.

Sommerville, C. John. *Popular Religion in Restoration England.* Gainesville: U of Florida P, 1977.

Swaim, Kathleen M. *Pilgrim's Progress, Puritan Progress: Discourses and Contexts.* Chicago: U of Illinois P, 1993.

Triefenbach, Peter. *Der Lebenslauf des Simplicius Simplicissimus: Figur–Initiation–Satire.* Stuttgart: Ernst Klett, 1979.

Waswo, Richard. *Language and Meaning in the Renaissance.* Princeton, NJ: Princeton UP, 1987.

Watt, Tessa. *Cheap Print and Popular Piety, 1550–1640.* Cambridge: Cambridge UP, 1991.

Index

Adam, 8, 24, 50, 52–53, 68, 83, 85–87, 118, 125
Adamic language, 66, 86–87
adventure fiction, 79
Albertinus, Aegidius, works by:
 Guzmán de Alfarache, 48
Alkon, Paul K., 111
allegoresis, 44, 66, 86
allegory, 3, 19–20, 23, 29, 31, 38–39, 41, 63, 115, 117, 136
Almond, Philip C., 6
Alpaugh, David J., 45
Alt, Johannes, 78
anecdotal literature, 131, 137
anecdote books, 137
anecdote(s), 73, 130, 136
Anglicans, 13, 30, 114
Arndt, Johann, 86
Arndt, Johann, works by:
 Paradies-Gärtlein, 124;
 Vier Bücher vom wahren Christenthum, 50, 82, 85, 87
Augustine, Saint, 50, 52
Augustine, Saint, works by:
 Confessions, 50
Augustinian tradition, thought, 1, 60, 77
autobiography, 9, 14, 16–17, 19, 39, 42, 50, 61, 67, 74, 83, 103, 122, 128, 135

Babel, 28, 66
baptism, 81, 84, 128
Baudach, Frank, 52, 77
Bible, 1–5, 7, 8–16, 18–20, 23, 24–27, 30, 33, 35–36, 38–45, 51, 55, 64, 69–71, 87, 89, 91, 96–101, 106–7, 110, 115–17, 119–20, 129, 135–36, 138
Bildungsroman, 61, 78
Blackburn, Timothy C., 112
Bloedau, Carl August von, 77
Blumenberg, Hans, 87
Böhme, Jakob, 6, 86
Book of Common Prayer, 3, 6
Book of Nature, 2, 53, 66–67, 86
Book of Revelation, 8, 24, 42
Breuer, Dieter, 77
broadsheet, 23
Browne, Thomas, 85–87
Brüggeman, Fritz, 120, 133
Bunyan, John, 1, 5, 8, 47–49, 89, 116–17, 120, 131, 135;
 secondary criticism, 32, 49;
 theology/doctrine, 7, 9–10;
 works of, 1, 4
Bunyan, John, works by:
 Grace Abounding to the Chief of Sinners, 1, 5, 7–21, 25, 27, 33, 44, 81, 82, 96, 119, 124, 135, 137; *The Pilgrim's Progress,* 1, 3, 5–6, 13, 19–20, 23, 24–35, 38–45, 47, 49, 51, 56, 58, 69, 71, 77, 80, 84, 89, 109, 111, 115, 117, 120, 129, 130–31, 135–38; *The Pilgrim's Progress,*

The Second Part, 1, 5, 23, 26–28, 32, 35–44, 71, 76, 120, 131, 135–36
Busch, Walter, 52, 77

Calvinists, 114
Campe, Joachim Heinrich, 79
chivalry, 23
chosen people, 8, 10, 24, 83–84, 118–19
Christ, 8–12, 15–16, 19, 24–26, 30, 32, 34, 37, 48–49, 68, 70, 81, 82, 86, 97, 100, 106, 135
Church of England, 13
civilization, 49, 51, 53, 83, 97–98, 100–103, 105, 108–9, 116–18, 121–22, 125, 127
Collins, Wilkie, works by: *The Moonstone,* 105–8, 112
communication, 2, 4, 8, 35–36, 44, 56, 71–72, 84, 121–22, 130, 139
communion of saints, 38, 81
communion service, 7
community, 5, 11, 13, 17, 23–24, 27–28, 34–35, 37–39, 43–44, 49, 71–72, 75–76, 123, 125, 128–29, 132, 136, 139
conversion, 9, 14–15, 17, 28, 30, 32, 34–35, 49, 52, 60–62, 65, 71, 75, 81–82, 84, 89, 96–98, 106, 122–24, 129, 135
conversion narrative, 17, 28, 30, 123–25
conviction of sin, 34
Counter-Reformation, 1, 2, 8

damnation, 12, 14, 16, 23, 42, 73, 75

Defoe, Daniel, 3, 48, 49, 51, 80, 108, 115, 117, 136, 137, 138; secondary criticism, 89
Defoe, Daniel, works by: *The Farther Adventures of Robinson Crusoe,* 105–6; *Robinson Crusoe,* 1, 4, 5, 7, 16, 33, 43, 44, 49, 51, 58, 63, 67, 68, 69, 79, 80, 81, 89–112, 115, 117, 120, 123, 131, 135, 136, 138, 139
Dent, works by: *Plain Man's Pathway to Heaven,* 17
desert island, 79–80, 83–84, 89, 91, 105, 110–11
devil(s), 18, 52, 57, 63, 90, 99, 100
devotional literature, 9–10, 17, 23, 48–49
doctrine(s), 9, 13, 14, 37, 41, 82; Calvinist, 10; Quaker, 30

earthly paradise, 37, 43, 83–85, 87, 90, 101, 117, 123, 125, 128
eighteenth-century literature, 80, 86
elect, 7, 9, 11–12, 16–17, 23–24, 26, 34, 37–38, 90, 109, 117–19
election, 7, 12, 16, 19, 26–27, 34, 37, 42, 44
Elizabeth I, 8
emblem(s), 31, 32, 41, 66, 70, 71, 80, 87; emblematics, 86; emblem books, 48
Enlightenment, 6, 89, 113
Erasmus of Rotterdam, 2
Eve, 8, 83, 118, 125
Everyman, 109

exemplary reader(s), 67, 71, 74, 137

fairy tale(s), 60
Fall, 8, 50, 62, 82–84, 86
fiction, 6, 20, 41, 44, 47, 64, 79–80, 107–8, 111, 115–16, 119–20, 131, 136–38
fortune, 61, 81, 83, 119
Fox, George, 86, 87
frame narrative, 113

Gaede, Friedrich, 77–78
Garden of Eden, 5, 87, 118
Gebauer, Hans Dieter, 78
Gerhard, Melitta, 78
German Romanticism, 113, 116
Gersch, Hubert, 68, 78
Geulen, Hans, 77
God, 1–2, 4, 8–13, 15–16, 18, 20–21, 24–27, 29, 30–31, 33–34, 41, 43–44, 50–55, 57, 60–62, 65–71, 80–86, 89–93, 96, 98–105, 107–10, 114, 116–21, 123–25, 131, 135–36, 139
grace, 10–12, 16, 18–19, 24–25, 29, 37, 45, 49–51, 84, 96–97, 129
Greaves, Richard L., 20
Grimmelshausen, Hans Jakob Christoph von, 3, 5, 47–49, 52, 61, 80, 89, 90, 115, 136–38; secondary criticism, 52, 60–61, 77–78; works of, 7, 44, 108
Grimmelshausen, Hans Jakob Christoph von, works by: *Der Abentheurliche Simplicissimus Teutsch,* 1, 4, 47–78, 79, 106, 120, 131, 136; *Continuatio,* 5, 47, 52–53, 60–62, 68, 73, 76–78; *Gaukeltasche,* 70–71; *Rathstübel Plutonis,* 76; *Der seltzame Springinsfeld,* 1, 5, 43, 47, 51, 61, 70–76, 78, 106, 136; *Simplicianische Schriften,* 76; *Das wunderbarliche Vogel-Nest,* 76
Gundolf, Friedrich, 78

hagiographic texts, 64
Haken, J. Chr. L., 132
Haller, William, 20
Hardin, Richard F., 45
heaven, 5–6, 10, 17, 19, 25–26, 42, 81, 119, 123, 125, 135
Heilsgeschichte, 25
hell, 5–6, 15, 124
hermeneutics, biblical, 8
hermetic literature, 86
hieroglyphs, 87
Holy Spirit, 3
Hunter, J. Paul, 89
Hutterites, 49
hypocrisy, 13, 28–29, 45, 59, 98, 121

imagery: sea, storm, shipwreck, 80–82
imagination, 44, 54, 62–64, 93, 95–96, 98, 108, 116, 131–32, 139
implied reader, 41
imputed righteousness, 11, 49, 96
ingenuity, 97, 102, 106, 108–9, 115
interviews, 28, 30, 31
Israelites, 10, 26, 107, 118–19

Jöns, Dietrich Walter, 87

justification of fiction, 47, 108, 132
justification of sins, 25, 30

Kayser, Wolfgang, 6
Keeble, N. H., 20–21, 45
Kempis, Thomas à, works by: *Imitation of Christ*, 48
Ein kurtzweilig Lesen von Dil Ulenspiegel, 136

Lalebuch, 3, 6, 136
Lamport, F. J., 120, 133
landscape, 23–24, 27, 39, 40, 44, 80, 83–84, 108, 116, 122, 127
law, 16, 24–25, 31, 55, 87, 118, 129
law of contraries, 93–94, 104, 123
Llewellyn, Terry, 78
Luther, Martin, 2, 10, 17, 20, 49–50
Luther, Martin, works by: *Commentary on Galatians*, 17
Lutheran(s), 8, 49, 114

Mack, Phyllis, 3, 6
marginal glosses, 5, 41, 42
Marryat, Captain Frederick, 79
mass, 7
Mayer, works by: *Verlohrnes und wieder gefundenes Kind GOttes*, 124
Meid, Volker, 132–33
memory, 16, 50, 51, 95, 98
Merrett, Robert James, 111
metaphor, 14–15, 39; digestion, 3; peach kernel, 53–54; pilgrimage, 23, 24; ship, 80; storm, 81; sugar-coated pill, 47, 54; wave and harbor, 125
millenarianism, 8
Moritz, Karl Philipp, works by: *Anton Reiser*, 133
mysticism, 2, 6, 86

Narrenspiegel, 70
natura integra, 50
Neoplatonic thought, 87
New Testament, 8, 9, 10, 15, 16, 24, 84, 119
Niclaes, Hendrik, 6
nonconformist(s), 3, 8–10, 14, 17, 20–21, 30, 32, 49
nonfiction, 130, 137
novel(s), 79; adventure, 79; desert island, 89, 111; early modern, 1; eighteenth-century, 79, 89, 105, 137; English, 89; history, development of, 61, 119, 132; picaresque, 48; theory of, 113

Old Testament, 8, 15–16, 20, 24, 84, 118–19
original sin, 24, 49, 52, 81, 84, 96, 124–26
Owens, W. R., 20

Pamela, 137
pansophism, 2, 6
pietism, 49, 113
pietist(s), 3
prayer(s), 54, 70, 97–99, 121, 133
printing press, 7
prodesse et delectare, 108, 115
prophecy, prophecies, 6, 8, 16, 59, 84, 94, 106, 121

Promised Land, 24, 26, 80, 83, 119
Protestant(s), 7, 8, 10, 48, 51–52
providence(s), 31, 80–81, 83, 90–92, 96, 98–99, 101–5, 107–8, 110, 114, 121–22, 128, 131
puritan(s), 45, 49

Quaker(s), 3, 13, 30, 45, 55, 120

Ransome, Arthur, works by: *Swallows and Amazons,* 109–10, 112
Ranter(s), 13, 14, 87
rationalism, 113
reason, 28, 51, 89–92, 96, 100–101, 103, 108–9, 113–14, 116, 118, 123, 138
Reckwitz, Erhard, 111
redemption, 8–11, 18, 23, 30, 35, 42, 52–53, 66, 73, 100, 125, 135
Reformation, Protestant, 1–2, 7–8, 20
reformers, English, 8
Reiss, Timothy J., 82, 87
Reitz, Johann Heinrich, works by: *Historie der Wiedergebohrnen,* 133
repentance, 24, 52, 71, 96–98, 100, 129
reprobate, 7, 10, 12, 24, 27–29, 32, 34, 40, 49, 90, 103, 106, 120, 124, 128–29
reprobation, 37
Restoration England, 17, 77
retrospective narrator(s), 4, 63–64, 67, 84
Rivers, Isabel, 45

Robinsonade, 79–87, 89, 111, 113–14, 123, 133
Rohrback, Günter, 78
Roman Catholic(s), 8, 48–49, 51–53, 69, 114, 126
romances, 49, 60
Romantic, 61
Rötzer, Hans Gerd, 77
Rousseau, Jean-Jacques, 79

salvation, 1, 5, 7–10, 12, 16–19, 23, 25, 27, 29–30, 32, 35, 38, 42–44, 49, 51, 53, 60, 66, 69, 71, 73, 75, 81–84, 90, 104, 118, 128, 131, 135, 138
satire, 48, 53, 62, 77
Saul, Nicholas, 132
Schmidt, Arno, 132
Schmitt, Axel, 77
Schnabel, Johann Gottfried, 3, 5, 48, 49, 79, 80, 89, 136, 137, 138; secondary criticism, 113, 120
Schnabel, Johann Gottfried, works by: *Wunderliche Fata einiger See-Fahrer,* 1, 4, 7, 24, 44, 49, 51, 79, 90, 100, 113–33, 135–36, 138
Scholte, Jan Hendrik, 76–77
Schwankerzählung, 136
Scripture, 2–4, 6, 8–14, 16–18, 23–26, 28, 30, 33, 35–36, 39, 44, 55, 95, 97, 100, 106–8, 116–17
sectarian(s), English, 3
Seidel, Michael, 111
Seven Champions of Christendom, 49
seven deadly sins, 51

seventeenth-century literature, 4, 48, 50, 80, 86, 89
Sharrock, Roger, 6, 20, 77
Sieveke, Günter, 78
signatures, doctrine of, 86
Smith, Nigel, 77, 87
Society of Friends, 86
Sommerville, C. John, 77
spiritual autobiography, 4, 7, 9, 15, 52, 60, 64, 80, 89, 107, 122, 137
Springer-Strand, Ingeborg, 132–33
Starr, G. A., 89
storytelling, 2, 5, 23, 35, 39, 43–44, 47, 61–62, 64, 67, 70–71, 73, 84, 101, 116, 125–30, 132, 135–39
Swaim, Kathleen M., 45
sympathetic listener(s), reader(s), 35–36, 72, 105, 126, 128, 130

Tarot, Rolf, 76
Ten Commandments, 49, 55, 118
theology, 18–19, 30, 100; antinomian, 13; Calvinist, 7; of divine grace, 50; New Testament, 24
Tree of Knowledge, 8
Triefenbach, Peter, 77
Tristram Shandy, 137
Trodd, Anthea, 112
typology, 8

Ursprache, 66
utopia(s), 52, 86, 114, 116, 133

Waswo, Richard, 6
Watt, Tessa, 45, 77
Weigel, Valentin, 6

Weydt, G., 77–78
Wharey, J. B., 6
Wimmer, R., 77
Word (of God), 10, 12, 26, 29, 38
Wycliffe, 49
Wyss, Johann, 79